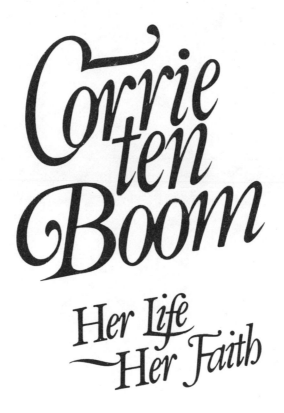

Corrie ten Boom

Her Life
~ Her Faith

Corrie ten Boom

Her Life
~ Her Faith

A Biography by
Carole C. Carlson

With a special tribute
by Billy Graham

Guideposts

CARMEL · NEW YORK 10512

This Guideposts edition is
published by special permission of
Fleming H. Revell Company.

Library of Congress Cataloging in Publication Data

Carlson, Carole C.
Corrie ten Boom: her life, her faith.

Includes bibliographical references.
1. Ten Boom, Corrie. 2. Christian
biography. I. Title.
BR1725.T35C37   1983   284'.2'0924   82–13330
ISBN 0–8007–1293–5

Contents

Part IV: Crossing Time and Space

Tribute to Corrie

Corrie's biography is more than the story of one woman. It is an example of how the Lord works in the life of a person who is surrendered to His leading and His will.

When I first met her in the 1960s, stories about her testimony of God's love in the midst of tremendous trials and the forgiveness He can give us for our enemies were beginning to follow her around the globe. I thought, *What an amazing sense of humor for a woman who has experienced poverty, the human hatred of Hitler's concentration camps, and the loneliness of always traveling and never having a permanent home.*

Little did I realize the impact she was to make upon my life and millions of others in the next two decades.

Her stamina astounded me. She could speak four or five times a day and counsel people in between sessions. She used every known mode of transportation, from elephants to rickshaws, to transport her with her gospel messages.

Ruth and I dubbed her "God's merry saint," and it suited her. Those unexpected flashes of humor could disarm the sternest and saddest heart.

There were times when we thought Corrie should slow down, but she possessed an intense concern for souls and for the times in which we live. She often told me that she didn't think the American people were prepared for suffering. She had an urgency to introduce more people to Jesus and to tell Christians everywhere to be ready for whatever might befall them, through storing His Word in their hearts and living each day as if the Lord would return any minute.

How can I measure the influence she has had upon me and my ministry? It is my prayer that her story, from her family foundations to her peace and constant joy in old age, will give strength to the readers of this book as she has given strength to me and my family.

BILLY GRAHAM

7

Introduction

When you met Corrie, you experienced her spiritual power. At first, it was difficult for me to relate to her. She seemed to live in another realm, where earthbound individuals were excluded.

Then two things happened that changed my relationship with this amazing woman and gave me the opportunities to write a book, *In My Father's House,* with her and now, to write about her. First, her secretary-companion, Ellen de Kroon, sensing how uneasy I was, said, "Carole, tease her." Corrie's sense of humor was always hovering near the surface, ready to explode. I learned to tease.

Next, I became sick while visiting her in Holland, and she was ill at the same time. While recovering in adjoining rooms in her house in Overveen, I learned that she was just as vulnerable as I. Consequently, I relaxed, and we became friends.

To write her biography took constant prayer, and I came to realize that many people who should be included in these pages would be left out. In corresponding with and interviewing more than a hundred people, I found many who were "Corrie's dearest friend." She had the gracious way of making each person in her life feel that he or she was the most important.

Among the many friends who have contributed to this biography are: Hans Moolenburgh, Ron Rietveld, Brother Andrew, Herman and Els ter Welle, Bill and Bettie Butler, Cliff Barrows, Hans Poley, Ben Hoekendijk, Sidney Wilson, Ellen Stamps, Edwin Orr, Jimmy Collier, Jeannette Clift, Katie Cheney, Harry Campbell, Jan van der Hoeven, Bob van Woerden, Harry Howard, Jamie Buckingham, Bill and Joan Brown, Peter van Woerden, Betsy Chapple, James Parker, Chuck Mylander, and all the wonderful people who wrote letters and sent tapes that contributed to the flavor of her story. Grateful thanks to my trusting editors, who believed enough in me to offer me this project.

To Lynne Dale, who typed the manuscript, and Ward Carlson, who prayed and encouraged me through the months of writing, I shall be eternally grateful.

To know Corrie is an emotional journey. Come experience it with me. . . .

CAROLE C. CARLSON

Prologue:
A Mystery

The guards were nervous. Their fingers tightened on rifles held tautly at their sides. In one of the largest prisons in the Philippines, an undercurrent of restlessness threatened to ignite the seven thousand inmates to violence. The night before, seven men had been stabbed to death with weapons devised out of parts of iron beds, honed into lethal daggers by being scraped on the bare, stone floors.

On the corner towers of the compound, machine guns were loaded, ready to halt any riot attempt. On the ground, an inadequate number of police were prepared for trouble. Adding to the tense situation was an insistent old lady who wanted to walk into this time bomb and preach!

Didn't she understand how desperate these men could be? Was she insane to think that her Bible and halo of gray hair could protect her from hardened criminals? How did she get in here, anyhow?

Holland was thousands of miles from Manila, but the reputation of Corrie ten Boom had spread to many corners of the globe. An unheralded missionary working in the Philippine Montinlupa Prison had heard that Corrie was going to be nearby and persuaded the warden to allow her to speak.

"You have my permission," replied the warden, "but only to talk to your Bible students."

The missionary was persistent. "But we can't invite Corrie ten

11

Boom for just a few men. She needs to speak to all the prisoners."

Considering the atmosphere in the prison, it was astounding that the warden agreed to the bold request. However, he allowed Corrie to come before the entire prison population, an unprecedented procedure in this institution.

The circumstances were grim, but Corrie lived above the barriers that would cause most persons to retreat. As she entered the long, stark hall leading to her command performance, she passed through a door with a sign that said SECURITY LIMIT.

"What does that mean?" she asked her escort guard.

"It means you take the risk, lady, if you go among the prisoners."

If she had any fear, it must have disappeared when she heard a reassuring sound echoing through the stone gray compound. The prison orchestra was playing:

> There is pow'r, pow'r, wonder-working pow'r,
> In the precious blood of the Lamb.

She had often said, "There is no reason to be afraid when a child of God has the protection of the blood of Jesus."

The musicians, provided with musical instruments by an American organization, World Vision, had been rehearsing for an important service. They had expected to precede the message of some booming evangelist from the States; instead, on came Corrie.

She walked up to the makeshift platform, maneuvering the steps in her slightly pigeon-toed gait, and looked at the sea of harsh and haunted faces. She noticed a few men with heavy chains on their hands and feet; these were the murderers. She was a curious person, seventy years old or more, with a nondescript print dress of uncertain vintage. She seemed to belong in a rocking chair, with knitting needles and a cat on her lap. What was she doing in this death trap?

Then Corrie experienced another miracle, which was the pattern of her life. Slowly she began to speak, the thick Dutch accent penetrating the shuffling, murmuring crowd until the men began to quiet down and listen intently. How could she understand their crying needs, their hatred and bitterness? How could this woman relate to the humiliation, the agony of being stripped of personal identity and self-worth? Yet, if she were crazy enough to come into this hellhole and talk to men who had given up hope of ever being more than animalistic, perhaps—just perhaps. . . .

She began to tell a story.

"During World War Two, in the town of Haarlem, Holland, my family and I hid many Jews from the Gestapo. My father was an old man, a simple shopkeeper in his eighties. My sister Betsie and myself were not too young, either, both of us in our fifties. For many months we housed a steady stream of Jewish refugee guests in our little house. We were a part of the underground movement in Holland, which was very dangerous—but somewhat exciting, too. For a while it was almost like a game, but we had no idea what a frightful game it was to become.

"On a cold day in February of nineteen hundred forty-four, there was a knock on our door, and the German police were there. We had been betrayed by two fellow Dutchmen, who delivered us into the hands of our enemies."

She paused; the men were listening in respectful silence. Betrayal was understood by prisoners; it was their existence, an ingrained habit in their savage world. They thought for such an action there was only one answer: revenge.

Corrie had their attention as she had had that of queens and commoners, professors and morons, society matrons and prostitutes throughout the world. She continued: "My sister Nollie heard of the trial of these two men who told the Gestapo about us, and she wrote a letter to both of them. She told them that through their betrayal they had caused the death of our father, our brother and his son, and our sister. She said we had suffered much, although both of us had come out of prison alive. She told them that we had forgiven them and that we could do this because of Jesus, who is in our hearts.

"Men, if you repent of your sins and come to Him, you will experience that our forgiveness is only a fraction of the ocean of love and mercy that awaits you when you come to Him as a sinner and receive Him as your Savior.

"What did we hear from the men who had betrayed our family? Let me tell you about the answers. One wrote, 'I have received Jesus as my Savior. When you can give such ability to forgive to people like Corrie ten Boom and her sister, then there is hope for me. I brought my sins to Him.'

"The other man wrote, 'I know what I have done to your family, that I have caused the death of several of you who have saved Jews, and above that I have helped to kill many hundreds of Jewish people. The only thing I regret is that I have not been able to kill more of your kind.'

"Both these men received the death penalty and were executed a week after they wrote those letters. One said yes to Jesus and one said no. Which are you? The Bible says, 'Make a choice whom you will serve.' "

Corrie's message was always simple, but profound. It was the story of God's love and the forgiveness He offered through Jesus Christ. She was told that two weeks after her prison talk in Montinlupa, a Catholic priest visited one of the death cells. He consoled the prisoner, "I am sorry that I must tell you that tomorrow at three o'clock, you are to go to the electric chair. Now, let us have a talk. You will soon come before the judgment seat of God. Do you confess your sins to me? I can give you absolution."

The prisoner answered, "I can't."

"Why not?"

"Because I brought all my sins directly to Jesus. He has cast them into the depths of the sea, and Corrie ten Boom says there is a sign: NO FISHING ALLOWED."

Twenty minutes before three on the following day, a phone call came that said the man had received a pardon.

The missionary who had invited Corrie to speak wrote her later that when she passed the Montinlupa Prison, she heard gospel songs everywhere. Whether or not there was a revival in this prison we may never know, but we do know that many men will share eternity with their friend, the funny old Dutch lady who in her lifetime ignored the security-limit signs the world had erected.

Why Corrie? Why did one woman, obscure and self-taught, confound some of the keenest university-trained minds? Why was she chosen to speak for thousands, to have her life exposed to millions through motion pictures, to be feted and awarded around the world? How could one human being's experience run the gamut from the extremes of filth and human degradation to a flower-filled suite at the swank Beverly Wilshire?

Corrie was not a Joan of Arc, a peasant girl who sprung from the earth, rootless and without family ties, or a Mother Theresa, a woman with a single, directed mission in life. Corrie was a merry saint who crossed time and space, a woman whose life was fashioned from her heritage. Why Corrie? Perhaps her past will speak to our future.

Part I

A Cloud of Witnesses

What can we learn from a legend? Are real-life heroes and heroines made of different clay from the rest of us? Corrie did not possess traits unavailable to other children of God, nor were troubles excluded from her experience. She had the same inner struggles we all have; for instance the need for a feeling of self-worth.

As we meet the cast of characters who influenced Corrie's life, we are impressed with the roles family members played in the life of this child. How did she learn to accept herself just as God made her? What happens when one person seems to have been shortchanged on beauty or charm?

Corrie discovered a universal truth when she learned that discipline and availability to God's direction—not good looks and intellectual prowess—are qualities for successful living.

The cloud of witnesses in Corrie's young life reveals the mystery of God's planning and timing.

1

God Uses Small People to Do Great Things

In the early nineteenth century Europe reeled under the onslaught of the little military genius whose conquests juggled thrones and kingdoms. The Napoleonic domination was not welcomed by some Hollanders, who remained loyal to the House of Orange.

To Gerrit ten Boom, "God, the Netherlands, and Orange" were praised in one breath. Dutch reverence for the monarchy went back to Prince William of Orange, who started the revolt against Spain that led to Holland's independence. Imagine, then, the turmoil in the heart of Gerrit when he listened to his own minister extol Napoleon and at the same time dilute the Word of God!

Gerrit was not a man to become easily upset. He was a deacon in his church, a man of prayer, and a staunch Dutch Calvinist. As chief gardener at one of the richest estates of Heemstede, he was a master craftsman in a respected occupation. However, he personally struggled against the spiritual coldness in his church, and on one particular Sunday the minister had gone too far! He not only altered the Bible to suit his own particular philosophy, but he also had some very appreciative words to say about Napoleon.

When church was over, Gerrit offered to drive the minister home to Haarlem. The ride from Heemstede was long enough to allow a good talk, and Gerrit was poised, ready to expound his convictions.

As the hooves of the horses clop-clopped along the flat roads, past the estates hidden by filigreed poplars and gardens that Gerrit scanned with a professional eye, he told his pastor exactly what he thought about the sermon.

"Pastor, you seem to have a very positive opinion about Napoleon. Most of us in the church are loyal to the House of Orange and the Dutch republic. . . . We may be oppressed by Napoleon now, but in our hearts we are free men. If you are unfaithful to the Prince of Orange, then one of us must leave the church."

Gerrit recorded this conversation in a diary, which was discovered over a hundred years later.

His anger seemed to build as he dealt his minister a final blow. "Furthermore, pastor, you face a severe responsibility when you place your philosophies above the Word of God."

When the two men arrived in Haarlem, the minister stepped down from the carriage, undoubtedly a bit shaken by the strong admonitions of his feisty deacon, and said, "Well, Gerrit, next Sunday I will do better."

Gerrit replied, "If God grants you the time to do so!"

Gerrit didn't realize how prophetic that statement would be. The minister died before the next Sunday arrived!

Gerrit ten Boom was Corrie's great-grandfather. Through his life, and for generations to come, we begin to see a thread of events that seemed to be part of a master plan which directed the lives of one insignificant family on the timetable of history. It is the story of simple people, living close to God, being molded for His work. Generations of war and gentle times, fierce hatred and fiercer love, reveal God's design visible in the cloud of witnesses in the ten Boom family.

After Gerrit's minister met his untimely death, a new pastor who believed in the Bible and stood against the tyranny of Napoleon was called to the church. Another act almost landed outspoken Great-grandfather Gerrit in the local prison.

Since it was forbidden, upon threat of jail or worse consequences, to speak against the Napoleonic regime, the new minister and Gerrit decided to show their defiance by singing the words of an old Dutch psalm that spoke of "the evil one" who runs around and stirs up people and holds the reins of government. Although the hymn was intended as a description of Satan, there was no doubt in the minds of the congregation that Gerrit and the pastor were singing about their political masters. News of ten Boom's traitorous deed was reported, and he received a summons to appear at the town hall.

Gerrit went before the authorities and compounded his record of insubordination by calling the arresting officer, Mr. Snotneus, which means exactly what it sounds like. If his employer, the rich merchant whose gardens he attended, had not interceded to have him pardoned (we can only surmise that Napoleon's men were not above bribery), Gerrit might have gone to prison. But God was not finished with him yet.

When Corrie was a little girl sitting on her father's lap and listening to the stories about her family, she was often told that God sometimes uses little events to change the direction of one's life. The spanking of a naughty child was the act that altered the ten Boom's careers and homelife for generations to come.

Gerrit, the proud gardener, was an artist who could coax strawberries to grow in winter and petunias and tulips to blossom in such profusion that the estate of his employer was a showplace of color and beauty. However, the little daughter of the owner was a spoiled child who deliberately pranced through the flower beds, destroying the careful planting done by Gerrit. After reporting this prank to her father, Gerrit was given permission to administer a spanking to the child if she disobeyed again. She did, was soundly paddled, and as a result harbored a lasting grudge against the gardener. When she grew up and inherited her father's estate, one of her first acts was to fire Gerrit, the longtime, trusted employee.

Gerrit moved his family from the beautiful countryside that had been their home for so long to the busy streets of Haarlem. One of his children, Willem, was delighted with the change, because he disliked gardening and loved the better educational opportunities in town.

The Bible, carefully read and well-worn, was the most important book in Gerrit's house. It was said that his home was a house of prayer and that many tears were shed for revival in his church in Heemstede. Almost a generation later, his prayers were answered as that very church became the center of an upsurge of faith in Holland —part of the Great Awakening in Europe during the mid 1800s.

When Corrie was more than eighty years old, she recalled a vivid dream she had about her great-grandfather Gerrit. She told me these details of the dream she had had when she was about eighteen.

Corrie dreamed she was in the old-fashioned kitchen of her great-grandfather's house. As they sat at the table, having some fruit grown on the beautiful Heemstede estate, Great-grandfather stood up, took her by the hand, and led her outside. "Come, Corrie, I want to show you the garden."

They walked together through a beautiful park, and Corrie recalled, "Great-grandfather talked about his flowers with great love. He told me, 'When you sow some seed and put it in the ground, this seed will make a plant, and this plant will give seed again. This will go on until the time when you will live, bringing more plants from this seed. You, my dear Corrie, are the daughter of my grandson, who is the son of my son. You are a plant, blooming from my seed.' "

Corrie continued, her memory sharp with the reality of the story. "We walked into the house again, and Great-grandfather said, 'Girl, I will show you something that will never be changed. It is the Word of God.' Then he opened his Bible, and I thought that was the most beautiful moment of my dream. He said that many, many things will be different, but this Book will be the same forever. He told me to plant the seeds from God's Book, and they will grow from generation to generation."

When Corrie spoke of her dream, the moment seemed mystical. If Gerrit ten Boom, the small, forgotten Dutch gardener, could speak to us from the past, he would probably quote the Psalmist:

> Listen, O my people, to my instruction;
> Incline your ears to the words of my mouth.
> I will open my mouth in a parable;
> I will utter dark sayings of old,
> Which we have heard and known,
> And our fathers have told us.
> We will not conceal them from their children,
> But tell to the generation to come the praises of the Lord,
> And His strength and His wondrous works that He has done.
>
> Psalms 78:1–4

In her life, which spanned two centuries, Corrie emerged as a woman who was a product of her heritage, strongly imprinted by her ancestors' lessons. Although Corrie may have romanticized the members of generations past, she never underestimated their influence.

2

I Will Bless Them
That Bless Thee

Willem ten Boom, Gerrit's son, was so cross-eyed that his wife told their children she was never sure whether or not he was looking at her. With such an affliction, it seems odd that the young Dutchman would become an apprentice in a watch-repair shop. Perhaps his attention to the minute workings of a timepiece could be centered more intensely when he focused one eye at a time on a problem.

The times in which he lived and raised his family were hard. Holland in the 1840s and 1850s was suffering from severe unemployment, floods throughout the precious farmland, and the havoc of potato blight. Also, there was turmoil within the churches. Many objected to a new law that made the king protector of the church, and others disliked the ideas that crept into church ritual, which were "not according to Calvin." A better life in America beckoned, and the first big wave of Dutch immigrants crossed the Atlantic between 1840 and 1860, many of them settling in Michigan, with its mighty forests, so unlike the flat grassland of the old country.[1]

If Willem had followed the mid-nineteenth-century emigration to America, as so many of his fellow Netherlanders did, the course of the generations to come would have been dramatically altered. But he chose to stay in Haarlem, operating his own watch shop on the Barteljorisstraat. This narrow little store, with its family rooms behind it, was destined to be made famous, through books and a motion picture, more than 130 years later.

Willem married Geertruide, who bore him thirteen children in the first fourteen years of their marriage. Eight of the children died in infancy, and continual bouts with illness and financial hardship built a strength of character that reflected in his spiritual life. In a fragile, yellowed letter found by his granddaughter, Corrie, years later, Willem wrote: "God has strengthened us during all these events. We have truly found that in Him there is grace and power. He is a solid rock in all our need."

When the ailing Geertruide died (undoubtedly worn out from childbearing), Willem married Elisabeth, who had been the housekeeper for the struggling family. Soon another child was born, a little boy named Casper. As he grew up, Casper began to hear the Word of God and daily prayers as a natural part of his childhood. Casper ten Boom remembered a portrait, imprinted on his child-hood memory, which hung in the living room. It was the image of an imposing man with kind eyes and a face that reflected strong convictions. His name was Isaac Da Costa; he was a Jew of Por-tuguese descent, a brilliant lawyer, and famous poet. Da Costa provided another link with history for the ten Boom family.

Theological thought was dividing churches and seminaries in Holland, as well as the rest of Europe. On one side were the liberal scholars from some of the major universities, who departed from belief in the infallibility of the Scriptures and that the Bible is the Word of God, to teach their own philosophies. One influential theological school of thought came out of the University in Gronin-gen. It taught, for instance, that mankind may become more and more like Christ and that religion has its source in a "special reli-gious feeling."

For several decades the Groningen school was extremely influen-tial, with its students filling pulpits and university chairs and active in home and foreign missions. The influence of liberal scholars at the University in Leiden spread these thought patterns into the provinces of tiny Holland, like a fast-spreading virus in a crowded schoolroom. Basic Christianity was being challenged; the battle lines were being drawn, and Isaac Da Costa became one of the strongest voices to challenge the dominant liberal theology of the time.

The tears and prayers of Gerrit ten Boom were being answered during the lifetime of his son, Willem, as Christian principles made some inroads into the social ills of the day. Holland began to experience a revival for which Great-grandfather had prayed, and it started in Heemstede, the very town where he had lived and worked. People came from miles around to hear a strong Bible-believing preacher, Nicolaas Beets; the ten Booms crowded into a carriage and traveled the muddy roads from Haarlem to Heemstede, to find the spiritual food that was missing in the liberal churches in Haarlem. Soon Christian organizations and missionary societies were formed, which reached out to the vast colonial territories controlled by Holland. More than in any previous century, Dutch Protestants began to spread the gospel news among non-European countries.[2]

As Willem was relieved of some of the constant burdens of a sick family, he involved himself in Christian outreach; he founded the society for Christian Home Visitation; he became an elder in the Reformed Church of Haarlem and began a fierce battle against modernism, rationalism, and unbelief, which were prevalent thoughts in most of the formal churches.

In the latter part of the twentieth century it is not unusual for Christian groups to pray for the peace of Jerusalem, or include concern and love for the Jews in prayer meetings. However, this was not the norm in Holland in the 1800s, so the formation of a weekly prayer meeting for Israel was marked down in the family history. In 1844 Willem began these sessions. Corrie wrote:

> We never know how God will answer our prayers, but we can expect that He will get us involved in His plan for the answer. If we are true intercessors, we must be ready to take part in God's work on behalf of the people for whom we pray.[3]

The seeds of love for the Jews were planted in the ten Boom family. As the prayer group continued week after week, year after year, the spiritual atmosphere of Holland began to improve. Isaac Da Costa, a Jew himself, spearheaded the movement that resulted in the formation of a number of similar prayer meetings throughout the Netherlands.

Seven years after Willem started his prayer meetings for the Jews,

Da Costa created a stir at the World Conference of the Evangelical Alliance, held in London. The Christian leaders in Great Britain had called leaders from many nations together, but ignored the nation of Israel. The fiery Portuguese Jew sounded a verbal trumpet before the nations of the world when he said:

> There is one nation which has not been represented at this great international gathering. It is God's own beloved people of Israel. Let us remember that our Saviour, the Lord Jesus Christ . . . was born a Jew in a Jewish family in the nation of Israel. It is true that Israel missed God's target and was, for a time, set aside and dispersed among the nations. But the day will come when they will fall at the feet of their Messiah in true repentance and live! . . . This is not human imagination, but God's own Word.[4]

Da Costa influenced Willem so strongly that he became a founder of the Society for Israel in Haarlem. He taught all his children a respect and love for the Jews, which they passed on to their children.

Willem was a student of the promises in the Bible; he knew the Old Testament prophecies concerning the return of the Jewish people to their homeland. The history of mankind until the middle 1800s recorded the wanderings of the descendants of Abraham, Isaac, and Jacob, a people with no country of their own, who suffered worldwide exile and persecution, just as Moses had prophesied when he said, "Moreover the Lord will scatter you among all peoples. . . . And among those nations you shall find no rest . . ." (Deuteronomy 28:64, 65).

However, the same Old Testament prophets who predicted the worldwide dispersion of the Jews also predicted their return.

As Willem's prayer group prayed for the return of the Jews to their homeland, word began to reach Holland about a movement, headed by the Austrian Theodor Herzl, to encourage Jews to return to Palestine. Although Herzl was motivated by economic and social survival for the Jews, he was, unknowingly, a key leader in the fulfillment of the prophecy that said, "then the Lord your God will restore you from captivity, and have compassion on you, and will gather you again from all the peoples where the Lord your God has scattered you" (Deuteronomy 30:3).

Corrie mused about her forefather's prayers for the Jews and the beginning of Israel's restoration, when she wrote:

> Is it presumptuous to think that the small prayer meeting in Haarlem was connected with these events? I believe that God delights to use His children in the fulfillment of His plans for the world. I am sure He loves to use small people to do great things.[5]

3

Beginnings in the Beje

Saturday night in the Beje (the nickname for that narrow, cramped house that was home and business for the hardworking ten Booms) must have been a rollicking event. The ten children Willem had from his two marriages were bathed in water that had been freshened with a dash of brandy. In later years, one of those children, Casper, wrote, "That particular smell and the fact that I received clean clothes made bath time a real treat."

Casper grew up in this atmosphere of hard work and few material comforts. As he matured, he began to be interested in spiritual matters; later Casper told his daughter Corrie that he had invited Jesus to come into his heart when he was about seventeen. When he was only eighteen he left home and went to Amsterdam, with no money and no business experience, to start a jewelry store in a very poor Jewish section of the city.

Casper became absorbed into the Jewish community, participating in their celebrations and holidays and beginning lifelong friendships. He also participated in a Christian outreach among poor people, which was called *Tot Heil des Volks* (For the Salvation of the People). Its headquarters is still in existence today, over a hundred years later.

One day the struggling young businessman met a dark-eyed,

soft-spoken girl who was teaching in a Sunday school. Cor Luitingh also knew what it was like to live in a large family and work hard for every necessity. Her father had died when she was very young, leaving her mother with a little store to manage in Amsterdam and eight children to raise. When Cor was in her late teens, she taught in a kindergarten run by her older sister, Jans, and another sister, Anna.

For Casper, it was love at first sight. When Cor went to the village of Harderwijk on the Zuider Zee, to visit her grandmother, the young merchant followed her and proposed. They were married in 1884 and settled in a small house in Amsterdam. Their life began in poverty and was plagued by debts and poor health, which for many people would be the basis for an unhappy home and a strained relationship. However, as Corrie wrote years later, "Father and Mother were close to each other, and they found that inner happiness does not depend on outward circumstances."

From letters and diaries kept by Casper and Cor, generations to come were allowed to glimpse the strength God gave them in their encounters with family and financial problems. Their first child, a happy little girl called Betsie, was born during the first year of marriage. Willem arrived two years later, and the beginning of Cor's bout with constant illness and weakness began. There were times when Casper sent her to the country to recover from yet another sickness. How he managed to keep his little jewelry store open, while caring for two toddlers, we can only guess.

The young father prayed for prosperity and healing for his beloved Cor, but added in a tender letter he wrote to her:

> But whatever the outcome, we shall thank Him, because all His doings are pure love. The important thing is that we live pure lives through His grace, that we grow purer, and that we come closer and closer to God. We must desire this with our whole hearts, for it is His will. I greatly long to have you home again and near to my heart, but if you need it, get more rest and stay until you are stronger.[6]

Casper was not immune to discouragement. As money problems increased he cried out in a letter to his wife, "I need to talk with somebody about my desperate financial situation." Another child, Nollie, was born in 1890, and the strain of childbearing and daily concerns took their toll upon Cor.

Casper wrote, however, in letters that were found more than eighty years later, "There is a divine plan behind it all, and through suffering, we will get to glory."

As the family grew, Casper had to find another house. His jewelry store was not in a section of the city where people could afford to buy his products. Fortunately, he found a place near the Queen's palace. The ten Boom family felt honored, indeed, when they were allowed to put a sign in the shop that indicated that they did work for the royal family.

However, life in Amsterdam was not easy for the growing ten Boom family. In 1885 and 1886 the vast unemployment led to riots in the working-class district of the city. Into this unrest stepped a self-proclaimed socialist who claimed to represent the working class. Domela Nieuwenhuis was a man with messianic visions, a former churchman who had turned to socialism with even more dedication than he had to Calvinism. This revolutionary infuriated the supporters of the crown with his insults against the royal family, and polarized much of the populace of the country.

It was at that very time that Casper put a sign in his shop which said *Hofleverancier* (one who serves the royal palace with goods).

A lovely little girl who was soon to become one of the most beloved monarchs in history, Queen Wilhelmina, spent some of her childhood hours near the jewelry shop. Her influence upon the ten Boom family was evident through two generations.

Wilhelmina had a personal sense of destiny from the time she was a young girl. Her insight into what she was being taught by her carefully chosen teachers, in contrast to the basic Christian beliefs that were instilled by her mother, gives us a key to the battle for minds that has been fought throughout history.

What molded the character of the child who was to reign for fifty-eight years over her strong, little country? What gave her the strength of purpose that inspired her subjects throughout the terrible dark years of enemy occupation during World War II? In her poignant autobiography she told of the mental and spiritual battle between the intellectual liberalism of the times and belief in a Creator God. In the latter part of the nineteenth century, Queen Wilhelmina wrote about some of her struggles with liberal teachers:

> Reason had the last word and in the final instance the attitude towards God and religious faith was one of negation. What could not be confirmed by scalpel, microscope

and telescope was denied and ignored. This spirit permeated the thoughts of many people without always mani-
festing itself directly. One felt it everywhere in the society
of the time . . . whenever God's guidance (as in history) or
God's omnipotence appeared to be ignored, I was hurt and
put up an inner resistance.[7]

How exciting it is to see the parallel between God's purpose for
the life of a queen and for one of her poor subjects. Wilhelmina
became a monarch who realized that it was God's guidance that
prepared her for the task of reigning through two world wars,
innumerable floods, and political unrest. At the same time she was
growing up, He was preparing another countrywoman who would
someday sit in the palace with her queen and share some of the
Lord's lessons.

But before all this took place, Casper was trying to balance business, family, and patriotic loyalties in Amsterdam, when he heard
that his father, Willem, was dying in Haarlem. Willem wrote in one
of his last letters: "I am living one day at a time. God's goodness is
eternal, and His faithfulness from generation to generation. I am so
much enjoying the presence of the Lord, and I wait for Him. My
suitcases are packed."[8]

Willem used his last strength to bless his son, Casper, like the
patriarchs of old; "The grace of the Lord Jesus Christ, and the love
of God, and the fellowship of the Holy Spirit be with you. Amen."

Today with such an emphasis upon "dying with dignity" we
could take lessons from those dear saints who have preceded us,
whose lives were lived so close to the Lord that when the time came
to leave their earthly bodies they could certainly say with the Apos-
tle Paul, "For to me to live is Christ, to die is gain."

In 1892, the ten Booms had a fifth child (one child died in infancy). To the impoverished family, already burdened with debts,
illness, and uncertain living arrangements, the arrival of a weak,
premature little creature must have been a blow. Her mother wrote
in a diary, "Oh, what a poor little thing she was. Nearly dead, she
looked bluish white, and I never saw anything so pitiful. Nobody
thought she would live."

Uncle Hendrik, Tante Jans's husband, saw Corrie and said, "I
hope the Lord will quickly take this poor little creature to His home
in heaven."

Corrie ten Boom began her existence on earth by amazing people. She never stopped!

When she was only six months old, a fussy, weak baby who spent most of her time tied in the apron of her mother's sister, Tante Anna, the family moved back to Haarlem. Casper was needed to manage the watch shop for his mother. A few years later, Casper moved his family into his childhood home, remodeling and enlarging the house above the shop by adding five small rooms on the third floor.

At that time Corrie was three or four years old, a delicate child with fears that made her shout wildly during the night, bringing her tired father hurriedly to her side to comfort her. In later years, those added tiny rooms became important refuges for others who cried in terror during the night.

So Corrie began life in the impractical house with its precarious, winding stairs and its growing tradition of love, pain, and outreach.

When the house was opened to the public in the 1970s and thousands of visitors tramped through it, many commented on how dark it was inside. But to Corrie it was a house of love and brightness.

The beginnings in the Beje prepared the way for light that spread around the world.

4

Love Story

The Dutch have a word that describes a home, a family, a feeling. It's simply *gezellig.*

Gezellig means "pleasant, cozy, and entertaining"; *gezellig* may also apply to a family that works and plays together, a family that lives in harmony and fun. It's what Corrie described in later years as the "art of living."

What a tribute it is to parents when their children see in them a love relationship that is strengthened by years of financial troubles and personal trials. Casper and Cor ten Boom had extremely limited material possessions, but a rich quality of life. Although their family was their first priority, next to their devotion to the Lord, they were not afraid to get involved with people who were in need. They shared their home, their food, their money, and their God with others.

Casper wrote tender love letters to his wife whenever she went to the country to recuperate from her frequent illnesses. One letter, which was found over eighty years later, began with an apology for not having written for three days!

I become more and more convinced that the Lord granted me an overwhelming privilege when He gave you to me. It may sound strange, but I think it is a proof of His great goodness that although He sustains me through so many difficulties, at the same time He causes me to be so thoroughly happy with you and our children. Perhaps the flame of my love may not burn as strongly as in the beginning. However, I can say that I have not abandoned my first love for you. It has never lessened. May the Lord grant that both of us may increase in love for each other and for Him.[9]

In an age of Victorian thinking, Casper was able to allude to a honeymoon passion in a manner that suited his gallant nature. As a gentleman of the old school, he referred to the more "delicate" subjects in terms that were appropriately dignified.

Casper's life reached far beyond the confines of his little home and shop in Haarlem. He studied and read in four different languages and attended international business meetings, where he was frequently one of the featured speakers. He was a gifted teacher, a great storyteller; Casper illustrated his talks with tales gathered from his extensive reading.

To know Corrie is to know her father. Although she loved and cared for her mother, it was the influence of Father that is seen throughout her life.

Casper was interested in every human being he met. His absorption with others often led to his disregard for some of the more routine matters of business, such as sending and collecting bills. He would repair a costly watch and then forget to set a price on his work.

He started each day in his workshop with prayer and Scripture reading, and all the family was expected to be there and on time. There was no excuse for tardiness.

The ten Booms were rich in many things. They were taught to love music and art. Within a short walk of their home were the galleries that displayed the Rembrandts, Vermeers, and Hals, along with others of the great Dutch masters. Music, especially Bach, was played, and songs and hymns were an essential part of family life.

But money? Every penny was turned, as the Dutch would say. When Corrie, Betsie, Willem, and Nollie were young, Tante Anna, the hardworking spinster sister of Cor's, worked night and day taking care of the children and nursing Cor. For her eighty-hour work week Casper gave her an allowance of one guilder (about thirty cents), each Saturday. By the middle of the week, finances would become so desperate that Casper would go sheepishly into the kitchen and say, "Anna, do you still have your guilder?"

The guilder was always available, and frequently it bought the food for the family that day.

Casper was a champion of the underdog. Whenever someone was being persecuted or treated badly, he rose to defend him. Once he was walking in the street and noticed a crowd gathering along one of the canals. As he approached the group he saw that a man on crutches, who was a worker in the Midnight Mission, a Christian outreach to prostitutes, was being taunted and cursed by some women from the red-light district. Casper walked over and stood with the missionary and began to take the brunt of the insults, too. He told his wife later that he believed he was in excellent company, because the Lord Jesus was a friend of prostitutes and sinners.

When Casper worked, he concentrated so intently that the household of women and children could swirl around him without distracting him. His watches ticked, his clocks chimed, and the little house rocked with babies' cries, women's voices, and smells of cooking. Until Willem was born, Casper was the only male member in a houseful of females. He was the head of the household, the intellectual and spiritual leader in his family. The most complicated bit of housework he ever did was to open and close the curtains.

From young manhood he began to grow a beard, and as the years passed he looked more like one of the Jewish patriarchs he loved to quote.

Casper was a craftsman, treating his fine watches with care and respect. People who walked into his workshop would often lean against the table and observe how precisely he cleaned and repaired a watch. It was like watching a fine artist paint a landscape or listening to a master musician. In the same way, his conversation was worthwhile, and he was ready to testify to his faith at every opportunity.

In the drawer of his worktable he kept a Bible, which was well-used. Casper used the Bible as his guide and always seemed to know the proper verse when someone came to him in need. Corrie asked him once, "Papa, do you learn by heart every text that you think will be useful for counseling people?"

"No," he answered, "it is the Lord who gives me the words I need."

He quoted Isaiah 50:4 (κjv): "The Lord God hath given me the tongue of the learned, that I should know how to speak a word in season to him that is weary. . . ." Isaiah was one of his favorite books and was read every Sunday during family devotional time.

Casper instilled in the minds of his family the importance of memorizing the Scriptures, a lesson that served his children well in the suffering times. He told Corrie, "Girl, don't forget that every word you know by heart is a precious tool that He can use through you."

The Word of God was in Casper's subconscious, and so were the languages he learned. He wanted his children to broaden their thinking outside of the little house in a small country; one method he used was to have Bible study in several different languages, simultaneously. German, French, English, Dutch, Hebrew, and Greek Bibles were used by different members of the family studying the same passages.

When Casper was in the latter part of his life, he became very ill and was taken to a hospital. Members of the family were allowed to stay with him during the night, and Corrie recalled that he became delirious and talked in mixed-up languages. Suddenly, however, he began to speak in French and gave a very lucid talk about teenagers who needed attention and how to reach them for the Lord. He had stored language knowledge in his subconscious.

Decades later, his youngest daughter used her language ability to reach many people all over the world with the love story of her Lord.

The battle for the minds of men is not a phenomenon of the latter part of the twentieth century. During the early 1900s, controversy whirled around the Bible as the Word of God, just as it does today. Casper had many friends who were agnostic, liberal, and socialistic, and he commanded their respect with his unwavering stand on the truth of the Bible.

When doubt began to corrode the faith of his only son, Willem, Casper was firm in his stand. Although Willem was grown and married by this time, Casper did not relinquish his role as the father who guides and admonishes. He wrote:

> Now you can be sure, Willem, that Bible criticism will bring death wherever it goes. Man's reasoning and the authority of the Bible seem to be irreconcilably opposed.

. . . The ground on which we build our hope does not lie
in man's knowledge, but in God's faithfulness. . . . We have
a clear choice between man's scientific criticism and the
declaration, "It is written."[10]

In the ten Boom dining room was a piece of furniture that was
the focal point for the family activity. The oval table, usually covered with a red and black cloth, was the gathering place for generations of aunts, children, visitors, and refugees. Eight decades later,
as Corrie established the first home of her own in America, a dupli-
cate of the oval table was searched for and found in a modern
California store. Around that original table in Haarlem began the
atmosphere of *gezellig* that wove its way into the life of the woman
destined to be loved by people in the nations of the world.

Corrie's character was shaped by the cast of players who contributed to the unending drama in the house on the Barteljorisstraat.
Her mother was a gentle, compassionate woman who brought harmony into the cramped quarters filled with divergent personalities.
She loved guests and had a gift for hospitality that stretched a
guilder until it cried.

Many lonesome people came to the Beje and found music, fun,
food, and interesting conversations. Cor kept a "blessing box" on
the oval table and would collect pennies or dimes in it for missionary projects. When a visitor arrived, she would spread her arms out
as if to embrace the world (not the visitor, this would be too forward
in their home) and say, "It's so good you are with us . . . a penny
in the blessing box for your coming!"

The soup may have been watered down, but the oval table always
had room for unexpected guests who came in just before mealtime.

In later years, when Corrie was traveling the world and dependent upon the invitations of other Christians, because she seldom
stayed in hotels, she was able to graciously accept food and lodging
from others. She said, "I think that I am enjoying the reward for the
wide open doors and hearts of our home. The Bible says, 'Cast thy
bread upon the waters: for thou shalt find it after many days' "
(Ecclesiastes 11:1 KJV).

Tante Bep, her face a picture of sadness punctuated by a tight
little bun on the top of her head, was the oldest of Cor's sisters who
lived with the ten Booms. She had been a nurse and went from
house to house, caring for the children in one wealthy Dutch home
after another. When she became too weak to continue in her profes-

sion, Casper and Cor took her into their family. Her irascible temperament must have been a challenge to the persuasive Cor, who had to still the troubled waters that Bep would stir. When Corrie would run to her mother, her feelings wounded by Tante Bep's caustic remarks, Cor would soothe her little girl and say, "Love her for what she is, Correman, and remember that she has had a very lonely sort of a life."

Tante Jans was a talented, opinionated woman, stern resolve showing in a solid jaw, with an attitude that put a strong period to every statement she made. She required special food, special rooms, and caused the house to buzz with her many projects. She was quite young when her husband died. Since she had no children of her own, she arrived in the Beje, bringing her furniture and many books; she was to live with the ten Booms until she died. The house was extended upwards, to give her more room.

"Corrie, Nollie, you are going to take music lessons. I have met a young soldier who is very talented, and I have engaged him as your teacher," Tante Jans would say. Her statements were decrees.

"The streets of Haarlem are full of young men in the service of the navy and the army. Idle minds make for mischievous thoughts. I am going to start a club for soldiers." And that's that.

Tante Jans was as immovable as her heavy writing desk. She marched to her own tune and spoke her mind on clothes, behavior, and theology. Casper believed in the grace of God and that the Bible says we are sinners saved by grace. Tante Jans believed that we are saved by works and that grace was a cheap way to salvation. Frequently Casper and Tante Jans would have lively discussions about their differences in belief.

Tante Jans, dogmatic as she was, showed Corrie and her brother and sisters an example of the gift of giving. She provided special treats when she received some unexpected income. The stodgy clothes she gave to the girls reflected her lack of taste, but somehow, with a ribbon here or some lace there, they managed to look stylish. The pictures in the ten Boom album always gave the appearance of a very affluent family.

Tante Jans was also an evangelist, with a real burden for souls. Corrie tells how from her earliest years she could remember Tante Jans's stories about people she had brought to the Lord. The whole family would rejoice when she told of another person who had accepted Christ as Savior.

Just prior to World War I, when the military was being mobilized,

she wrote Christian tracts that she had published and gave to the
soldiers. In one of them she wrote:

> Have you never introduced Jesus to someone else? Then
> I doubt that you know Him. Jesus has said, "Also I say unto
> you, Whosoever shall confess me before men, him shall the
> Son of man also confess before the angels of God: But he
> that denieth me before men shall be denied before the
> angels of God" (Luke 12:8, 9).

This tract was passed out to many soldiers, who spent four long
years at the borders of neutral Holland, during World War I. Perhaps it was from Tante Jans that Corrie learned the value of tracts
and the example of personal evangelism.

Corrie's aunts were characters. To describe Tante Anna is like
moving into a warm kitchen and sampling freshly baked bread. Her
heart was as ample as her girth; her round face reflected compassion.
She was Corrie's substitute mother whenever Cor was too ill to care
for the family. She ruled her little basement domain with creative
hands, stretching little to make much. Tante Anna had her Bible
studies, too, particularly among the servant girls who worked in the
homes of the wealthy Dutch merchants. Every Wednesday and
Sunday evening some of the girls would meet in a club room or at
the Beje for some sewing and Bible study. She taught them gospel
songs and thought of many of them as the daughters she never had.
When one of her "children" went astray, she became so upset that
she would cry for hours. Casper would console her by saying,
"Anna, you cannot bear these burdens all yourself. Cast your wor-
ries upon the Lord."

Tante Anna, devoted and generous, dedicated her life to her sister's family and the needs of her girls. She knew the results of a
morally decadent world through her ministry with her servant girls,
who frequently became sexually involved with someone. It was
sensitive Anna who taught Nollie, Betsie, and Corrie the "facts of
life," which Corrie remembered in later years as the most difficult
task Tante Anna undertook.

Years later, after Tante Anna had died, Casper told Corrie, "Once
Anna told me that she would never marry, because the only man
she ever loved was me." Remembering her growing-up years, Corrie
had difficulty conceiving of the fact that her beloved aunt, living in
proximity to him in such a small household, was secretly in love

with her father. That she suppressed this emotion was a credit to the tenderness of a servant's heart.

One thing that Corrie learned from Tante Anna was the joy of being a part of family, although unmarried herself. Corrie also learned to cook and stretch a little into more. Her cooking school was a perch beneath the table in the small kitchen, where she listened to the conversations and watched Tante Anna bustle about her pots and pans. When Corrie was old and fame elevated her to a position where she was expected to be an expert in everything, she was asked to provide her favorite recipe for a cookbook. She began with simple ingredients: "Start the day by praying and reading the Bible." Then she gave her famous culinary triumph: creamed endive, prepared with three heads of endive, two tablespoons of flour, a half cup of milk, and a half tablespoon of butter.

Caring for Tante Bep, Tante Jans, and Tante Anna, nursing them when they were old and feeble, taking financial and personal responsibility for members of the family are qualities that were accepted in the home of the ten Booms in the early 1900s. The elderly were not put in old people's or nursing homes; they were kept in the family. Decades later, when Corrie was old and helpless, that same tender care was returned to her.

When the children were growing up, Nollie was strongest of the three girls. She was only a year and a half older than Corrie, but was a *moedertje* (little mother) to her. She held her hand protectively, when they went outside, and calmed her fears by allowing her to clutch her nightie when they went to bed. The bedsteads were made of iron, sturdy and lasting as the Dutch, and the mattresses were thickly stuffed with feathers, meant for comfort and warmth in the poorly heated house. Every morning it was Nollie and Corrie's job to stand on each side of the bed and fluff the mattress and covers.

More than half a century later, it was Nollie who had to write Corrie that their beloved father had died. Again, it was the "big sister" who remained such a source of strength for Corrie. She wrote her:

My Dear Kees [Corrie's nickname],
. . . Darling, now I have to tell you something very sad. Be strong. On the tenth of March, our dear father went to Heaven. He survived only ten days. He passed away in Loosduinen. Yesterday I fetched his belongings from Scheveningen. I know the Lord will help you bear this.

Nollie was always there giving Corrie the hand to hold in the dark.

When Corrie and Nollie were small, they played together in the street beside the house, which became their yard, their training ground for life. In that alley they met the drunks being propelled by the police to the jailhouse a block away; they encountered the poor and the neglected and learned to care for the less fortunate. In later years Corrie's love of the outdoors and her raising her face to the sun for a permanent tan must have evolved from the lack of sunshine in a Haarlem alley.

Growing up with Betsie, the oldest of the ten Boom girls, was a lesson in charm. Betsie was the beauty, the little lady. Corrie was afraid to play with Betsie's doll because it was always well dressed and immaculate, just like Betsie. Her doll was named Emma, after the mother of the beloved Queen Wilhelmina; Corrie's doll was named Casperina, after her father. Casperina had a cracked head from being dragged up and down the stairs and had a few fingers missing. When Casperina played with Emma, it was like a poor servant girl sitting at the table of royalty.

Betsie had curls, Corrie's hair was straight. Betsie was delicate, a fragile cameo among the jewels of the watch shop. Corrie, after her weak start, became a solid, sturdy little mischief maker, clop-clopping her way into one prank after another. Betsie was the pet of the family, frail in health, but talented in art and beauty. She was a clever raconteur and could weave an original and humorous story out of the mundane happenings in life.

Betsie never married, although her beauty attracted many young Dutchmen. As the years passed and Corrie and Betsie lived many new roles in their life's experiences, they melded into a partnership in which the talents of each complemented the other. They functioned as a team that was to touch the lives of millions outside that little corner house.

Corrie learned the love of colors, flowers, and beauty from the sister who never lived on earth to see the results of her amazing influence upon her little sister.

Brother Willem was woefully outnumbered in the houseful of women and girls. However, Casper brought his son up with wisdom, instilling in him a love of learning and a sense of a Christian's responsibility toward the Jews. When they were young, Willem guided Corrie in language study, urging her to expand her abilities in more than one language.

Willem's scholarship and vision were influential in later years, when he began to examine the subject of anti-Semitism. He studied the undercurrent of thought patterns in the European literature of the nineteenth and twentieth centuries, which indicated the trend toward treating Judaism as a racist subject instead of a religion. Many intellectual writers in France and Germany were laying the insidious foundation for the Holocaust by saying that the Jews were an inferior race.

Willem's concern for the Jews, from the biblical and historical viewpoints, gave Corrie much of her personal understanding and compassion. After he had married and established a rather secure position as the minister in a church, Willem was asked to take a job as a missionary to the Jewish people in Amsterdam. The cycle of the family was coming around full circle again. Casper wrote to his only son:

> . . . . My father, who was a great admirer of Da Costa, was a lifelong member of the Dutch Society for Israel. A portrait of Da Costa hung in our living room for as long as I can remember. A large number of workers for the cause of Israel have visited our home. When I lived on the Rapenburg in Amsterdam, I often used to speak to the Jews about the Messiah.
>
> But all this is not the main thing. The most important matter is that for many years you have had a great love for the Hebrew language and now, through your response to the present wave of anti-Semitism, you have discovered in yourself a special love for God's own people.

In those frightful years of World War II, the turning point in God's direction for Corrie, her brother Willem was one of the guides in the underground activities of the family. From childhood to maturity he had a strong intellectual impact on Corrie.

Environment is not the only influence that molds a human being. Out of the mire may emerge a godly saint, used by God to enrich the neighborhood or world in which he lives. However, with Corrie, the pattern of her heritage and family can be seen in the tapestry of her life. The teaching she received was in daily living. In the Old Testament, Moses told the people of Israel about the commandments of God and said:

So keep these commandments carefully in mind. . . .
Teach them to your children. Talk about them when you
are sitting at home, when you are out walking, at bedtime,
and before breakfast! Write them upon the doors of your
houses and upon your gates, so that as long as there is sky
above the earth, you and your children will enjoy the good
life awaiting you in the land the Lord has promised you.

Deuteronomy 11:18–21 TLB

Gezellig is the description of the ten Boom life. Love is the emotion
that dominated the many faces and ages which spilled out of that
narrow house with its open doors.

5

Don't Cry, Corrie

Childhood memories touched Corrie's adult experiences in many ways. When Casper tucked Corrie into bed, his beard tickling her chin and smelling faintly of Dutch cigars, he would place his hand gently on her face. Oh, she didn't want to move—he might leave the room, and then she would be alone in the dark. But if she began to whimper, his tone would become firm. "Be a big girl, Correman, don't cry."

Corrie remembered her father's hands when she was in prison camp; she could feel them on her face, comforting and protecting her. Father gave her strength, just as her heavenly Father sustained her throughout her life.

One time, when she and Nollie were small, they were knocked down by a man on a bicycle. Both of them ran into the house, covered with mud, displaying scraped elbows and knees. Nollie screamed so loudly that Mother and Father gave her all their attention, but Corrie retreated to the corner, remembering that Father had said, "Don't cry, Corrie." Then Mother spied her and cried, "*Hemeltje* [little heaven], come look at Corrie!" Corrie blinked back the unwanted tears and wiped her bloody cuts, trying to be the "big girl" Father told her to be.

Another time Corrie was the ringleader in a school prank. When

Corrie attended school in the early part of this century, any insignificant infraction of classroom protocol called for disciplinary measures, perhaps even being expelled.

She was about ten years old, a student in a Christian school that her father had helped start, and was already exhibiting the leadership that was to be one of her lifelong attributes. One long afternoon, when the hours seemed to stretch ahead interminably, the teacher left the room just long enough for Corrie to rally all sixty schoolchildren behind her plan. Although it was against the rules to wear a cap or hat in class, she intended to lead a minor rebellion by urging all the pupils to put on their hats at exactly two o'clock. Since she was the only one who had a watch, she was to give the sign.

As the countdown began, the room was unusually quiet, which to any teacher is an ominous sign. At the zero hour, Corrie reached under her desk and plopped on her head the large blue and white sailor hat that Tante Jans had given her. At that moment, Mr. Van Ree, the stern teacher, returned, looked at her, the only one wearing a hat, and said, "Go to the headmaster at once, Corrie ten Boom!"

Tears began to dim the twinkling blue eyes as she realized that none of the other children had followed her lead. She had to stand alone in her humiliation. What would Father think? Would she be expelled for her behavior? "Don't cry, Corrie," must have echoed in her ears.

Corrie told Nollie about her dilemma that night as she crawled into bed and pulled the feather comforter up to her chin. Nollie, with all of the wisdom of the big twelve-year-old sister, said, "Do you remember that boring Psalm that Papa read to us, where every sixth or seventh verse said the same thing? '. . . Then they cried unto the Lord in their trouble, and he delivered them out of their distresses' " (Psalms 107 KJV).

Corrie told me, seventy years later, that she remembered "crying unto the Lord" and being able to go to sleep with the assurance that the Lord would make everything all right. She was not expelled from class, and the headmaster let her off with a comparatively mild admonishment. "Corrie ten Boom, I don't think you behaved as a very good Christian girl yesterday."

For Corrie, crying was a sign of personal weakness. However, time and cruel circumstances softened her stoicism. A lifetime later, Corrie unleashed some pent-up tears caused by the memories of harsh years. As she viewed a motion picture of her life, she weaved out of the private screening room and was enveloped in the big, black arms of Ethel Waters, a woman who also knew hardship and tragedy. Corrie, the old soldier in her eighties, wept like a child as another great servant of God held her and sang, "His eye is on the sparrow, and I know He watches me."

Corrie's lifelong love for music was nurtured in her childhood. Her indomitable Tante Jans guided her into singing in public; her first performances were for the Dutch soldiers. Corrie recalled that military people were brought in off the streets, and she and Nollie were called upon to entertain. One sergeant was a fine musician, so Tante Jans had him give the sisters lessons on the harmonium. When Corrie was only twelve years old she accompanied the hymn singing and joined in duets with Nollie.

One evening, in Tante Jans's living room, filled with overstuffed and oversized furniture, Corrie sang about the lost sheep who was found by the shepherd. It is a credit to her remarkable memory that many decades later she remembered the last line. She sang, "And that sheep that went astray was me."

Poor little stray sheep. It must have seemed very unlikely to the worldly-wise soldiers that this sweet-faced little girl knew anything about "going astray." One tall, burly officer lifted her on his lap and asked, "Tell me, how did you go astray?"

Corrie confessed that the words just belonged to the song and that she couldn't remember any experience of being lost and then found by the Shepherd.

As she grew into her teens, her gospel singing took her into larger and larger groups of people. She was not without fears and stage fright, for she wrote to one of her friends:

> . . . I have a small part in the glorious work of bringing the Gospel to several hundred people. Sometimes I stand there with my heart beating wildly and my voice trembling. . . . At those moments, it is such a comfort to me that God's strength is made perfect in weakness. . . .

The first few years of the new century were calm ones in Holland. Queen Wilhelmina was on the throne, a woman with deep spiritual values and a strong sense of destiny. It was during this time before

World War I that the beloved monarch was growing spiritually, evaluating her personal relationship with God.

The Queen and the commoner, one of her loyal subjects who would later play an important part in her life, were maturing in their relationships with their Creator in such a way that when they were old, God brought them together in a unique way.

In her autobiography, Queen Wilhelmina has given us some insight into the personality that later made her a symbol of Dutch pluck and unity. She wrote about her growing faith:

> Truths that for many people do not become living reality until they are much older, God made me discover at an early age, through struggle and resistance against the unacceptable, without human help, all alone, yet not alone, for there was always His powerful invisible help. . . . In these years a deep desire was fulfilled for stability, for a profounder spiritual life, for a conscious union with God in Christ. This desire was so strong that the performance of my task seemed impossible to me without its fulfillment.[11]

Another Dutch girl, insignificant in the world's eyes, but important in God's sight, also struggled against the unacceptable. One of the most difficult trials in Corrie's teenage life came when she was ordered to bed for five months. For a seventeen-year-old, full of life and spunk, the doctor's diagnosis was like a death sentence. They thought she had tuberculosis, which at that time was a dreaded affliction that could mean months, sometimes years of bed rest.

"Don't cry, Corrie!" What foolish words in those circumstances. Her family consoled her, but she saw only injustice in the diagnosis. She indulged in self-pity, realizing that the long walks, the gymnastics, the life jammed with activity would be denied her.

Corrie had been taught to thank God for all things. She heard her father thank Him when the bills came and there was no money; she heard her mother thank God when she could add a little water to the soup and invite someone to dinner. But she couldn't thank Him for making her an invalid! Her meals were brought up to her; she was not allowed visitors, except for the family; and life was miserable.

During the forced inactivity in her little room, Corrie began to study church history, upon the urging of Willem, who was then a theological student at the University of Leiden. After five long months it was discovered that she didn't have tuberculosis after all, but an infected appendix. She had a minor operation and was able to return to the outside world. However, her confinement as the result of that wrong diagnosis "worked together for good" to give her a background in biblical history that she might not have had otherwise.

When Corrie was strong again, she began to develop the natural restlessness of a teenager to "experience life." Her world had been limited to the streets of Haarlem and an occasional trip to Amsterdam with Father. She began to worry that her family would think she was ungrateful if she expressed the desire to leave home, so she took her problem to her Bible teacher, Mrs. Van Lennep, who proved to be an understanding woman. "Corrie, it's very natural for you to feel the way you do. You can do something in the world through the power of the Lord."

One of the jobs that a poor, but respectable, young woman could fill was that of *au pair* in the home of a wealthy family. Since Corrie had experience and diplomas in home economics, child care, needlepoint, and similar subjects, the job of governess or companion for children was a natural one.

Her first job was a test of her personal attitude and moral strength in facing a home and life-style that were alien to her upbringing.

Corrie left the small, crowded rooms of the Beje for a house in which the living room alone was as large as the ten Boom's entire first floor. Although her employer's home was only ten miles from Haarlem, in Zandvoort, a lovely village by the sea, it seemed to Corrie that her new residence was in another country.

First, she discovered that social position, clothes, and possessions were priorities. The little girl she was to teach was unruly and undisciplined. Corrie said, "If I had acted as she did, I'm sure I would have been expelled from school."

However, the greatest shock to Corrie, at the innocent age of seventeen, was the attention she received from her employer.

She remembered the very words he used as she recalled, almost seventy years later, that first venture into the outside world. One day when her rebellious little charge was napping, Corrie was walking down the wood-paneled hall in the bedroom wing of the mansion, when her employer, a portly merchant, encountered her. "Corrie," he said with a slight whisky breath, "I'm an old goat, but old goats like young, frisky female goats."

Poor, sheltered Corrie, with little or no instruction in the ways of the world, escaped into her room and "cried unto the Lord," just as she had done with Nollie when she was small. She was disillusioned with wealth, social position, and men. She didn't want to go home, because she wasn't a quitter, but she lived from Thursday to Thursday, when she had her day off and could return to Haarlem for her catechism lesson. This new adventure in living turned into a trip into darkness.

One day Willem came to visit her with the news that their oldest aunt, dour Tante Bep, had died, and that Tante Anna was suffering from extreme fatigue as a result of the responsibilities of nursing Bep in her final years. Corrie had to stifle her elation over the news. It wasn't really proper to be happy that her aunt had died, but it gave her the logical reason to leave her job and go home.

Home! How wonderful it looked! The small, cramped rooms, the shabby furniture, and the love. The harmony of the Beje was such a contrast to the strife and ugliness in the mansion by the sea. Corrie realized why Tante Bep, who had spent many years of her earlier life as a governess in the homes of the rich, had developed such a cynical personality.

Corrie had her taste of life beyond Haarlem and decided she didn't like it. She probably never told her father about the Zandvoort episode, since "such things" were not discussed in their home. The sex instruction that Corrie and her sisters received was from blushing Tante Anna, who had never been married. However, Corrie could not hide her troubled face from her discerning father. He told her, "Don't forget, Corrie—underneath us are the everlasting arms . . . we have God's promise of security when His arms are beneath us . . . holding us . . . supporting us . . . strengthening us."

Casper ten Boom provided the direction for his children in all their learning experiences. He pointed them toward God's strength, when their own ability was inadequate.

In later years, after a lifetime of traveling, suffering, and living, Corrie wrote in a book of daily devotions:

> God gives us two types of guidance. The first is unconscious, and comes because our lives are committed to Jesus. The second is special guidance, for instance when God

wants to move us in a new direction—a new job or a new field of work.

She quoted Psalms 32:8: "I will instruct you and teach you in the way you should go; I will counsel you with My eye upon you."

After the disastrous *au pair* episode, Corrie did receive that "special guidance." The year was 1910, and she was a wiser, more mature eighteen-year-old. In Holland, as in the rest of the world, it was a time of optimism, of belief in a better world and in man as an ethical being who could not only materially relieve the needs of the underprivileged classes, but also enrich their minds. Corrie was intelligent enough to discern that the idea that the world was going to get better and better was a fallacy; however, she needed to find out for herself, and when she heard that a Bible school was going to open in Haarlem, she was excited.

Corrie never did one thing at a time, even as an emerging young woman. She enrolled in seven different major subjects in the Bible school: ethics, dogmatics, church history, Old Testament, New Testament, Old Testament history, and New Testament history. School was not a full-time endeavor, but what she undertook after completing the many chores of the household; her extracurricular activities were assisting Tante Anna in the housekeeping, cooking, cleaning, and nursing chores.

Corrie said she was not a "clever student," yet I have observed a woman whose ability to astound some of the keenest minds of our time has been shown in her books and public appearances. However, her sprightly good humor showed through her account of the Bible-school examinations.

There were two parts to the final exam: The first part was an interrogation by students, which she breezed through; the second section was more formidable. A group of ministers gathered in a conference room in the stately cathedral, St. Bavo's. The stone walls of the impressive church were never warm, and the afternoon of the examination they seemed unusually chilly. Corrie suddenly discovered that she was being questioned by two pastors who had a personal feud over theological disagreements. The atmosphere became so tense that she failed all seven of her subjects.

Corrie went home, dejected over what she thought was a pattern of defeat that plagued her young life; however, Betsie would not tolerate such an attitude. She told her, "When you have failed an examination, Corrie, you must take it again until you succeed and have your diploma."

She did take the examination again—eight years later—and passed. Whether it is a Dutch trait or a personal Corrie ten Boom attribute, stubborn persistence became a pattern in her life.

6

What's Wrong With Me?

In her teens Corrie was a reticent romantic. Although life in raw reality was unacceptable in her sheltered upbringing, the gossamer love stories of a Victorian era were her secret fare. She read novels in three languages, imagining herself as the heroine, not as a victim of evil motives.

From the time she was fourteen, the main hero in her fantasies was a tall, blond friend of Willem's. He was an "older man" of nineteen when Corrie fell hopelessly in love. The first time he seriously noticed her was when she and Nollie traveled to the University of Leiden to visit Willem. Nollie, with her soft dimples and pale, upswept hair, was the center of attention whenever the opposite sex was present; but Corrie, with the awkward gait and careless dress, was the funny little sister who sparkled with mischief. However, when Karel paid more attention to Corrie than he did to Nollie, the seal was stamped on Corrie's heart. He was the man for her, and for seven years she tucked his image into the recesses of her imagination, knowing that someday the time would be right for God to bring them together.

Meanwhile, there was so much to do, so much to learn about the world beyond the borders of the Netherlands. The ten Boom household was a place where missionaries and watchmakers from other lands came to visit; with them they brought stories of contrasting cultures and expanding ideas. In a time when radio and television were not available to release minds from the confines of one's own environment, this little family was encouraged to stretch their out-reach.

In her late teens, Corrie began to meet people in missions work from all over the world and talk with Christians from other denominations. Were there really other doctrines than those in the Dutch Reformed Church? It was exciting to talk with people from other countries and to discuss different viewpoints of theology. Corrie wanted so badly to "be somebody," to learn all she could and experience more of life. Haarlem was comfortable, home was secure, but she was always on the search for something more, for adventure without risk.

When she was about nineteen she met a strange man who had become a legend throughout the European Christian community. His name was Sundar Singh, and he was born into a wealthy Sikh family in India. As a child he had been taught to hate Jesus, and he burned every Bible he could find. He threw mud on the Christian missionaries who came to his town and shouted obscenities at them.

However, Sundar Singh had an urgent desire to know God. He was a restless young man and prayed that if God really existed, he wanted a sign that He was there. The story is told that this Indian, like Saul on the Damascus road, saw Jesus and heard Him say, "How long will you deny Me? I died for you; I have given My life for you."

The young Indian testified that he fell on his knees before the Savior and accepted Him as his Lord and Master. He wove some Indian mysticism into his Christian ideals, and therefore, was given the title of *Sadhu* (Indian holy man) Sundar Singh.

When Corrie heard that he was going to speak at a weekend conference near Lunteren, she packed her rucksack and blanket and went to the campgrounds, although she had not made a reservation. "I can sleep in the field," Corrie pleaded, "I would just like to attend meetings with the Sadhu."

The young student who admitted her to the conference was named van Hoogstraten. He became a missionary himself and had a daughter, Conny, who, years later, was to be Corrie's first companion in her travels around the world.

During the weekend when Corrie listened to the Sadhu speak, she became very disturbed. He told of visions and claimed to have seen

Jesus face to face. Corrie began to wonder if her relationship with God was as deep as it should be. She left the camp and started to walk through the heather, so absorbed in her thoughts that she didn't notice the man who was walking toward her. Suddenly she stood face to face with Sadhu Sundar Singh.

"Please, Mr. Sadhu, tell me what's wrong with me? I'm a child of God, I have received Jesus as my Savior, and I know that my sins are forgiven. I know He is with me, for He has said, 'I am with you always 'til the end of the world.' But I've never seen a vision or experienced a miracle, as you have."

This Christian mystic from India answered Corrie with words she remembered all of her life. He told her that people came to him to see a miracle, but he would send them to Corrie ten Boom, a young Dutch girl from Haarlem, who had never seen Jesus, but knew Him because she had accepted Him as her Savior. He told Corrie to look up John 20:29, which says, ". . . Blessed are they who did not see, and yet believed."

"Corrie," he said. "Don't pray for visions; He gives you the assurance of His presence without visions."

In years to come, Corrie did have visions and experienced miracles. However, they did not seem to be experiences she sought, but rather a growing relationship with the God she loved, which made some of the happenings in her life appear almost mystical.

Corrie returned home after her encounter with the Sadhu, full of the excitement of her experience. Sharing was an integral part of her family, especially in the deeper meanings of spiritual life. Father was always attentive when his children and friends told of insights into biblical truths. Frequently he would say, "Isn't it wonderful to have such joy here on earth? It's a little foretaste of heaven. Yes, the best is yet to be."

Corrie learned from her father the lesson of listening. One of the great secrets of her ingratiating personality in her mature years was the intense interest she had in all people.

The year was 1916 and changes were being made; Willem was going to be married, and more important, Karel would be at the wedding. Corrie was more grown up now, with more knowledge of life. Betsie made her a beautiful silk dress for the wedding, the elegant material having been purchased through the sacrificial money from Father's giving up his cigars and Tante Jans rationing the coal in her room.

The wedding of Willem and Tine was beautiful, but few people realized the soaring hopes in the heart of the youngest ten Boom. Corrie was in love! Surely Karel must have felt the same way, for in the months to follow they met frequently for long walks through the countryside. As the young couple talked about the future, Karel's call to the ministry, his ambitions to have an affluent congregation and a large old manse, the conversations seemed to include a wife and a family. Corrie realized that marriage was never mentioned, but the implication seemed quite clear, at least to her.

Older brothers may dampen the dreams of their younger sisters, and Corrie did not want to accept some of Willem's gloomy remarks. "Corrie," he said seriously, "you don't understand Karel's family. They are very ambitious, and they have worked and planned for Karel to marry someone with prestige and influence. Don't let him break your heart, Corrie."

Corrie's nature was too sunny, too positive, to listen to some of the doomsday predictions of studious Willem. In those days he talked so much about war and politics that he was unpleasant to be around. Corrie's world was bathed in fun, music, and dreams. The world was rumbling all about, but Corrie, like Holland, was a neutral land surrounded by the guns of war.

Looking back on history, it is difficult to understand how the Dutch people could have been so insulated from the signs of smoldering relationships that surrounded them. Queen Wilhelmina wrote in her autobiography, "The outbreak of the war came as a complete surprise to our unsuspecting people. In those days even the better-educated were ill informed about political questions outside our frontiers."[12]

Holland, although maintaining its neutrality, began to mobilize. Regular soldiers and reservists were called up, and family life was disrupted throughout the country. In addition, thousands of refugees began to pour into their tiny country as the Germans invaded Belgium, bringing both civilians and soldiers flooding into Holland. Food and housing had to be found for all the additional people. And as World War I stretched over the years, Holland suffered severe shortages.

War tensions, which were intensified during the years between 1914 and 1918, reflected in the lives of everyone. A nation may be neutral, but at heart, man is never neutral.

In the midst of all of the misery caused by the war, the Netherlands was ravaged by extensive floods; heavy storms sent the water pummeling the dikes of the Zuider Zee, and many of them collapsed or overflowed. Food became so scarce that the ten Booms, along with other poor Dutch families who lived and worked in the villages or towns, were making soup with one turnip and stretching a guilder until it hurt.

In 1917 there was new hope for an end to the dreadful war. The United States joined the Allies, and soon troops and supplies began to appear at the front; gradually the news began to come through that the German army was in retreat and the war might soon be over.

However, for Corrie the most exciting news was a letter from Karel, telling her about his new parish and his wealthy congregation. It must have seemed to her that the ambitions and dreams they had shared in those lingering walks were coming true in a rush. But then her world crashed: The war that swirled around the borders of Holland was no less intense than the battles in her heart on the day she flung open the door of the Beje to encounter a sober-faced Karel, with a lovely, fashionable girl clinging to his arm. "Corrie, I want you to meet my fiancée."

Her family came to her rescue, making the proper conversation and serving coffee as Karel introduced them to the young woman who was to be his bride, a girl from an influential family, just as Willem had predicted.

What could Corrie do? She was not a child with a scraped knee who was told, "Don't cry, Corrie." She was a girl with a broken heart and a hurt that could not be kissed away, even by Papa!

Corrie, in some prophetic insight, knew that there would never be another man to love in the same way she loved Karel. But how could she bear the rejection? Father's soothing hand rested on her sobbing head, tenderly stroking the cheek of the daughter he loved so much. "Corrie, love is the strongest force in the world, and when it is blocked that means pain.

"There are two things we can do when this happens. We can kill the love so that it stops hurting. But then, of course, part of us dies, too. Or, Corrie, we can ask God to open up another route for that love to travel. Ask God, Corrie, to give you His love for this man, a love nothing can destroy. Whenever we cannot love in our own human way, God can give us the perfect way."

All of her life, Corrie retained the childlike faith she had in her earthly father and her heavenly Father. It was during that dark moment in her young life that she began to learn the lesson that carried her through times when to love on a human level seemed impossible.

More than forty years later she wrote: "Trustingly I put my hand in His hand, like a sad child who knows his father does not make mistakes."

In 1920, Corrie told her father that she wanted to work in the shop with him. Father said, "Then you must have the best education. When you can make something, you can repair it." Consequently, with one small valise containing a change of clothing and her Bible, Corrie embarked on an adventure that was preparation for her unique occupation of watchmaker.

Young ladies from Holland in the first part of the twentieth century were not businesswomen. Class distinctions were emphasized, and people were addressed according to social rank. Consequently, for the poor, but proud, ten Booms to allow their protected, childlike Corrie to go to Switzerland to learn the watchmaking trade was a very liberal attitude. Dutch historians tell us that during that time the compartments for female passengers on the first- and second-class carriages of the railways were marked LADIES, while the third-class carriages were labeled WOMEN.[13] Knowing the character of her father, we surmise that Corrie was sent on her long journey to Switzerland in a railway car for LADIES.

When she arrived in Basel, she had her first experience in a hotel. She looked at the doorman and wondered if she should tell him where she was going. After all, that's what she did when she went for a walk at home.

When Corrie began to work in the Swiss factory where she was to be an apprentice in the art of watch repair, she soon discovered what it was like to be a cog in a machine, not the center of a loving family's attention. Her job was to place curves in spiral watch springs, nine hours a day, six days a week. Her young muscles strained to be active; her eyes longed for relief. One day a large dog ran into the factory room, and Corrie dropped her work to indulge in a laughing, tugging romp with the lovable animal. Flushed and disheveled, Corrie looked up from the floor to see the factory owner staring at her with disapproval. Oh, no, here she was again, caught by a stern teacher and about to be sent to the principal's office.

But Corrie was becoming bolder and less inclined to be intimidated. She told the man that it was the fifteenth day she had been making curves in spiral springs and, "Your dog was a most welcome guest, perhaps he saved me from going crazy."

The director was not sympathetic. He told her that he had spent nine hours a day for two years, making that curve. Corrie thought that was dreadful; she understood discipline, but the Swiss seemed to carry it to an extreme! They had such a strenuous schedule and demanded such exactness from the workers! What possible good could come out of this rigid, dull training?

Many years later, Corrie was a factory worker again, this time in a German prison camp in Vught, Netherlands. Her routine was: sit with others in a row, put together parts for German airplane radios, learn to live with dullness and routine. From prison Corrie wrote her family a sentence that epitomized her life: "We are in God's training school and learn much."

7

The Years Between

Victory in war carries harsh consequences. Although the Allies had defeated German militarism and dictated severe peace conditions, the results were costly. Many lives were lost, immense amounts of money spent, and Europe suffered from a lengthy and painful economic crisis.

In the ten Boom household, many changes were taking place. Willem was married during the war, and Nollie became a bride in 1919. The Beje seemed to be emptying quickly.

As the aunts and Mama became more infirm the care and nursing of these elderly loved ones occupied the continual attention of Corrie. With the weakening of their bodies, the testimonies of their lives were intensified.

For Tante Jans, the powerful evangelist, teacher, and Bible study leader, as age and her diabetic condition forced her to retreat to her rooms, the fear of death became more acute. The reason for her anxiety was attributed to her lack of salvation assurance. The ongoing theological argument that she had with Father was summed up in the text ". . . work out your salvation with fear and trembling; for it is God who is at work in you, both to will and to work for His good pleasure" (Philippians 2:12, 13).

Tante Jans emphasized that we should work for our salvation

(therefore she was never sure she was good enough), while Casper believed that God is at work in you when you accept Jesus as Savior and commit your life to Him.

Corrie thought these two views were contradictions in logical thinking and knew that Father was right. A short time before Tante Jans died, a great peace came over her. She, also, accepted Christ's assurance of eternal life and said to Corrie, "Isn't it good that Jesus has said, 'I give my sheep everlasting life?' " And that was the text, from John 10:28, which marks her resting place.

Three years before Mama died she suffered a severe stroke that left her completely paralyzed. Her gentle voice was quieted, but her sweet and loving spirit strengthened the family. Corrie, full of energy and zest for living, said that she hoped the Lord would never make her so completely helpless.

The crowded little house seemed so empty after Mother and the aunts had gone to be with the Lord. The trays, the bedpans, the running up and down the stairs for the needs of the sick and the weak ceased, and two young women and their father remained. It would have been so easy and so natural, to slide into a comfortable routine of the house, the shop, and the Bible studies. Certainly having children in a house that had been full of the elderly for so many years would be a contrast in life-style.

But the children began to arrive. First, some undernourished, frightened little German boys and girls, uprooted from their homes by the war, were brief guests in the warm little Haarlem house. Their stay was considered temporary, although it did stretch into many months. As they cared for these children who were broken in body and spirit after the burden of war and death, Corrie thought, *O Lord, don't ever put us through that in Holland. I don't think I would have the personal strength to watch my own family suffer.*

When the German children left, restored in health, the seed had been planted for children's voices to vibrate through the old house. Corrie cleaned the little rooms that were once so overcrowded and thought of a plan that Nollie, Betsie, and she had dreamed about when they were girls. She had said, "Mom, when we are grown, we will give rooms to missionary children. So many cannot stay with their parents on the mission field, and the children have to sacrifice because their parents are obeying a call from God. Some will understand this, but others may resent it."

Mother was delighted when Corrie told her that, because she did not want her own children to be missionaries. However, to care for children of missionaries seemed to her to be a noble calling.

Corrie found herself facing the reality of her childhood fantasies when Willem visited the watch shop one day with an urgent request. As the pastor of a struggling church, Willem had been instilled with a desire to help missionaries. He felt that the Lord wanted him in Holland, but his interest in world affairs propelled him to serve on boards of various organizations that supported missionary activities. One of these was a Dutch East Indies mission that supplied funds and encouragement for those people who brought the Gospel to remote areas. Willem presented his request to Corrie, Betsie, and Papa ten Boom at the oval table in the dining room, where many decisions were made throughout the years.

"It has just come to my attention that there are three children of missionaries who need a home immediately. Their parents must leave for the mission field and have been praying for families which are intellectually inclined to take them for a time. I thought this might be something for you."

Willem was not a person for subtlety. He presented the problem, then gave the solution; his direct manner was both an asset and a liability. However, he understood his family, and he knew that when they were confronted with a human need, their response would be quick.

"We can find a home for the boy, but we need a place for the two girls. This is a faith mission. When the finances of the mission are good, you will be paid. If there is nothing, then the foster parents must live on faith, like the missionaries."

Living by faith for finances was not a new concept for the ten Booms. After Willem had left, Corrie said, "One girl could sleep in Tante Bep's room." Father peered over his wire-rim spectacles and said, "So, you are already arranging the house. Well, if you two agree, I will not refuse, but let us pray about it first."

The next day the director of the mission visited the watch shop and said, "We have thanked the Lord that you are willing to take the two girls."

Father didn't seem to be upset about such a presumptuous prayer, because he answered, "Of course, if you have already thanked God, we cannot refuse. When can the children come, that we may see them?"

Within a short time, the two sisters and their father became the foster parents of all three missionary children, including Hardy, the boy. Although he was scheduled to go to another home, they could not bear the thought of separating the brother from his sisters.

Puck and Hans, the sisters, were bright little girls, eleven and twelve years old; Hardy was a serious young man of fourteen. The sounds of the Beje changed overnight from the quiet ticking of the dozens of clocks and the hushed singing of hymns to the rollicking treble of young voices and feet.

As a result of the influx of children a new direction was launched in the life of Corrie. In the next few years the narrow little house on the Barteljorisstraat burst with eleven foster children; there were as many as seven living there at one time.

The old house became rather crowded. Once a missionary's daughter was on her way from Indonesia to Holland, but just before the boat left, the uncle with whom she was to stay sent a telegram saying that she was not welcome. Another missionary said, "Send her to the Beje, they always have room. If they don't, they will make it." Even the name, Beje, came from the missionary children. They were unable to pronounce Barteljorisstraat, and gave it the shortened version, Beje (pronounced *bay-yay*). Decades later that name was made famous in books and films throughout the world.

Betsie took care of the cooking and clothing, and Corrie specialized in the sports and music. These activities at home provided the springboard for clubs that eventually expanded into a worldwide Girl Guide movement.

In perspective, as we watch the expansion of interests and activities of Corrie, it becomes apparent that no circumstance is too insignificant for God to use in the lives of His children.

Corrie was thirty-three years old when Hans, Puck, and Hardy came into her life. God had shown her years before that marriage and children were not a part of His plan for her. However, in an unheralded way, she began to promote a family life that gave her many children.

Over fifty years later, Hans, who was a bright, perceptive child, recalled those early years in Haarlem. She is now Mrs. A. Kappner-Van der Veen, and lives in Geldrop, Holland. "I know that we lived in the so-called crisis years. People lived in a more simple way then, and I think this was also very noticeable in the watch shop, because if one has to economize, the luxury articles are usually the first to be left out. Life was sober in the ten Boom family, but very happy. They knew how to enjoy all the little things of life.

"In 1925 we came to live with the ten Booms. I remember mostly that Tante Kees [Corrie's nickname from the time she was ten years old and a tomboy. *Kees* is a boy's name.] sincerely enjoyed life, as did Tante Bet. They enjoyed every small thing intensely, because they believed that everything is given to us as presents from God.

"I remember one of Opa's favorite hymns: 'Ik heb de vaste grond gevonden' [I have found the sure foundation]. I think this indicates the source from which they lived. Please don't think that it was an overspiritual life all day long. We had great fun together.

"After the war, I often thought, *Corrie's whole life has been a preparation for the 'big' work she has done since.* However, in recent years my thoughts have been that the work she did in the 1920s and 1930s was important, too. She gave to many girls what is most precious for this life, for they might never have heard the Gospel if it hadn't been for her.

"Corrie was blessed with many talents. She herself would say, 'Those are things one cannot make oneself, therefore thank God for the gifts you have received.' I believe that it is very appropriate to thank God for all the gifts He gave to Corrie ten Boom and for everything we have heard and learned of our heavenly Father through her."

Scores of people attest to the influence upon their lives of Corrie ten Boom. During those "years between," the seemingly drab years in the life of a person whose later adventures were so colorful and dangerous, there were hundreds of young people who found direction for their lives through the influence of Corrie, Betsie, and Father.

Hans, Puck, and Hardy were instant family for the sisters ten Boom and Papa. The temporary arrangement grew into many years, and Hans said that during the years she spent in the Beje, she grew from a child into a young woman. She wrote, "I still often thank God that He gave me these substitute parents when my own parents were in Indonesia as missionaries and that I was privileged to live with the ten Booms during those important years."

Bent over his papers from all over the world or repairing the intricate workings of a fine watch, Papa disregarded the noise and confusion of the youthful activities that surrounded him. He was also blind to their faults and pranks. He boasted, "Our children are such good kids, they never quarrel!"

Corrie, who was the disciplinarian, might just have sent one of the children to her room for sassy behavior. She would march upstairs, probably with heavy, resounding steps, since Corrie carried some solid Dutch weight, and confront the culprit with his or her sins.

A frequent expression Corrie used was, "We must remember that the children were born after the Fall." One of the foster children, Puck, remembered one of her frequent closed-doors talks when she had told Tante Kees that she hated Lessie, another foster child, and was admonished, "Puck, don't you know Jesus says that hatred is murder in God's eyes? He told us that we must love even our enemies."

Puck, sitting defiantly on a little bed, with Corrie looking directly into her glasses, smudged with angry tears, heard the message Corrie repeated around the world.

"Don't you know, Puck, that in Romans five, verse five, Paul says, '. . . the love of God is poured out within our hearts through the Holy Spirit . . . ?' If you give room in your heart for the Holy Spirit, He will give you His kind of love, a part of the fruit of the Spirit. And that love never fails."

"But Tante Corrie," Puck objected, "what must I do? I have such hateful thoughts in my heart."

"John says, 'If we confess our sins, he is faithful and just to forgive us our sins, and to cleanse us from all unrighteousness' [KJV]. Jesus will cleanse your heart with His blood, and then He will fill you with His love. Shall we go to Him now and tell Him everything?"

Years later the little missionary girl, Puck, was tortured in a military prison camp in Indonesia. She told Corrie, "Often when I was being beaten, I thought of you and Opa and remembered what you had taught me about love for my enemies."

In our jet-propelled society, with computerized living and split-second scheduling, we often think of people who lived fifty years ago as leading a slower, more relaxed life. Corrie worked in the watch shop, cared for all of the children, conducted Bible classes in public schools, and taught Sunday school. One day Corrie was confronted with another need. She was attending a lecture by a lady from the *Union des Amies de la Jeune Fille* (Union of Lady Friends of the Young Girl). Corrie was not at ease with these wealthy society women; although clothes were never very important to her, the contrast between her short-sleeved blouse and nondescript skirt and the beautiful peau de soie gowns of other women caused her to retreat into the corner of the opulent drawing room. She heard them talking about the great need for club activities to fill the gap between Sunday school, which ended when the girls were twelve, and the YWCA, which was designed for young women. Teenagers did not have much to occupy their spare time.

"Corrie ten Boom, that sounds like work for you."

Corrie tried to ignore the finger that was poking her in the arm. Mrs. Bechtold was a dear old lady, a friend of Tante Jans who knew the ten Booms and Corrie's abilities. *Oh, no,* thought Corrie, *not another thing to do!* She used the classic excuse of the ages, "I don't have any time."

"Pray about it," whispered the insistent lady.

That evening Corrie talked it over with the Lord, and as a result, the youth clubs were born. She sat at the oval table, wondering where to start on this project; she had no money, no place to meet, and no experience. One of her favorite Bible verses was: "By faith Abraham . . . obeyed; and he went out, not knowing whither he went" (Hebrews 11:8 KJV).

Casper knew many wealthy people in Haarlem, since he repaired their clocks for many years. Armed with the names of his affluent clients, Corrie started on her quest. "Mrs. Van Gelder, I would like to ask you a favor. We are going to start a club for some girls who need recreation and some instruction from God's Word. May we use a corner of your garden to entertain the girls, play games, and give them a Bible message?"

Corrie obtained the use of the grounds of many magnificent estates; it was difficult to refuse her direct requests. She and Betsie began to gather the names of girls, which wasn't difficult to do, since Betsie had taught Sunday school for many years. Soon they had so many girls it was obvious that they needed to divide responsibilities and have leaders. Corrie began to use her business to prospect for young women she could train for her team. When a young woman came into the shop with a watch to repair, Corrie launched into her approach. When she found a likely candidate, she would talk about her concern for girls between the ages of twelve and eighteen and invite her customer to come to a meeting for potential leaders.

Within a short time she had gathered forty leaders. Corrie laid out a simple plan, and the clubs were launched. Each week the club leader chose a bridge in Haarlem for the meeting place. They would gather and then walk to the garden of some estate for games and talks. It was exciting because the girls would find out the location of the club meeting when they arrived, and it was novel.

However, August arrived, and it was an unusually rainy month. The leaders stood on the bridge, waiting in vain for the girls to arrive. Only a few bedraggled souls came, and spirits were pretty low.

However, Corrie took it to the Lord in prayer and asked for a room in which to meet. Corrie's determination said, "Does your faith move mountains, or do mountains move faith?"

She went back to her wealthy friends, more confident now of the Lord's leading and less intimidated by their jewels and silks. "I asked you for a corner of your garden before; now I come to ask for a corner of your purse. We have many girls who need activities and the love of the Lord, but we also need a room so they will not be just fair-weather friends."

The *Union des Amies de la Jeune Fille* was willing to form a board to back the club work. First a room was found on the Bakenessergracht, a canal near the Beje. When the shop was closed and supper was over, it only took Corrie a few minutes to run to the meeting. However, soon the room was too small for the growing clubs. The leaders prayed every week for larger quarters, and soon their prayers were answered. A very large and well-known house was made available to them, and soon the Teyler house, named after a well-known Haarlem philanthropist, was bursting with music, singing, folk dancing, sewing, handicrafts, and gymnastics. From a poke in the arm, when one elderly lady said, "Corrie, that's work for you," to the burgeoning clubs was just a short time. Corrie was God's servant for this insignificant movement that multiplied into a worldwide organization, but the forgotten women attending a tea in a Dutch drawing room were equally being used for God's purpose.

The foster child Hans wrote about those years in the clubs.

> Corrie had definite leader's capacities, without being overpowering. She always discussed things with the team of leaders and was the cheery center, without being dominant.
>
> She organized many clubs. Everybody called her Tante Kees. She was so well-known that one day the mailman

brought her a postcard that was addressed: "Tante Kees, Haarlem."

The purposes of the clubs were to bring the Gospel to the girls and to keep the girls off the streets. From a one-night-a-week meeting, the clubs grew so that they were meeting every night. At each meeting, three to five minutes were spent talking about the life of Jesus, a Bible story, or an application of the Gospel. If the girls wanted to know more, they could join a confirmation class, which prepared them for membership in the Dutch Reformed Church.

Each year the club girls had a festive evening and program in a theater. Every club did a skit, musical, or country dance. The girls marched forward in formation, and when they were all on the platform, Corrie came and opened the evening.

One talk she gave at one of these occasions was titled "God's Telephone Is Never Engaged." Another year it was: "Do You Have Your Radio Tuned in on the Right Station?" Hans wrote, fifty years after participating in these programs, "I can still see her standing there. It made a real impression on me and no doubt on others, too."

Corrie, with her Victorian upbringing, needed a guardian on the board of the *Union des Amies de la Jeune Fille*. A doctor's wife was given the responsibility of seeing that Corrie did not carry some of her ideas and pranks to an extreme. Consequently, when the revolutionary idea of a club with mixed groups was considered, Corrie had to be very circumspect. *De Vriendenkring* (the Club of Friends) was started, and the experiment was kept quiet for an entire year. The secretive side enlarged the interest. Corrie told about the fun they had in this club and said, "I do not believe we had any evenings with the same program."

Sometimes they talked politics, other evenings they went for rowboat rides on the River Spaarne. Once they decided to climb the cathedral tower. For boys and girls in their late teens, this was no insurmountable feat, but for Corrie, who disliked heights, it was a major accomplishment!

One young man in the club, who was an undertaker, used the hearse to go driving with his girl friends on Sunday. On Monday, it might have the sober job of transporting coffins. One girl after another rode through the countryside in solemn style, but no one would marry him. Corrie had to counsel him about his mode of transportation.

About forty years later she was in Holland between her trips around the world, and in a church she met the undertaker, who said, "Don't you know me? In your *Vriendenkring* I found the Lord. The knowledge of eternal life has been the strengthening force in my life and my profession."

Corrie did not discourage romance in the Mixed Club and was always so happy when some of her young men and women were married.

Sunday was always a consecrated day of rest in the ten Boom household. However, for Corrie, Sunday afternoon became a time when she had "church" for the feebleminded. When she had a girl or boy who wanted to join the clubs, or when she was told by the pastor of a person who was disrupting the church service, Corrie invited that individual to her "special" church. She wrote in her little book *Common Sense Not Needed:*

> I started a work to bring the Gospel to feeble-minded people who were not in institutions. They were not able to go to church; they could not understand the sermon. But did they not need the Lord Jesus, just like you and I? We learn from the Bible that the Lord Jesus has a great love and concern for everyone who is in need.
>
> . . . this small work was perhaps unimportant in the eyes of the world, but not worthless in God's eyes. No effort can be valueless when it is in obedience to the command of Jesus, "You must go out to the whole world and proclaim the gospel to every creature."

As Corrie worked with the bright, challenging foster children who lived in the Beje and kept up with the mental and physical gymnastics of her teenage club children, she also met weekly with the feebleminded, Mongoloid, and low IQ people.

One of Corrie's stories about her Sunday-afternoon church group is simple, and poignant:

> Kareltje was a little boy, twelve years old. He had blue eyes and curly hair. He was one of a large, poor family, and his father was cruel to him, because Kareltje was feebleminded. He listened as I told the story of the disciples giving food to five thousand people. As the five loaves and

two fishes passed from Jesus' hand to theirs, the bread and fish became sufficient to feed the multitude.

Suddenly Kareltje jumped up, and swinging his arms around him cried, "There is enough! There is plenty for everyone! Just take as much as you like!"

Kareltje felt himself one of the disciples. What a joy! "Plenty for everyone!"

I wished every child of God rejoiced as Kareltje did about the plenty that we have, when taking all from Jesus' hands and passing on to others."

Corrie knew that the Holy Spirit doesn't need a high IQ in a person in order to reveal Himself. It was this concern for the feebleminded that infuriated the Germans, who had been indoctrinated in the belief of their superior race.

Corrie began her camp and conference life during those years when the clubs grew to great numbers. During the summer she arranged for times when the girls and their leaders could come together in the outdoors. First, the outings were done with tents, and later a building was found and dubbed *Bliscap*, which was an old word for "joy." It was a simple log cabin with room for about sixty girls.

The intimacy of camp living promotes the dangers of gossip, so one of the articles in the camp law was: "If you must tell something negative about someone else, first tell ten positive qualities about him." If anyone made a gossippy remark during a meal, someone simply said, "Pass the salt, if you please."

Those camps and the simple lessons Corrie taught remained indelibly stamped on the lives of "her girls." The highlight of each day was the campfire, at night, when the girls sat in a circle around the fire, blankets over their shoulders, and sang. Hans wrote, "Tante Kees gave the evening meditation, and these were times we never forgot."

Corrie was famous for her exciting stories. She would exercise her lively imagination to conjure thrilling tales. The last evening at camp, however, was very special. When everybody was in bed and the lights were out, Corrie would creep out of the window and sing a good-bye song in her warm, contralto voice.

Another club girl, Pussy, now Mrs. Rie Droog, of South Africa, reminisced about camp life. She said, "I have known Corrie since

I was fourteen. I am now seventy-one. I first met her at the Haarlemse Meisjes Club (HMC). I attended the common club, gymnastics, and catechism; at the end of the latter I was confirmed in the Grote Kerk of Haarlem. At that time her club girls nearly all belonged to the working class, so they were not spoiled. The years between 1928 and 1940 were hard, with very much unemployment. I also attended several camps with her and even made a tour along the Rhine, by boat and on foot.

"At night we had a campfire, and we listened intently to all Tante Kees said. Her simple way of storytelling deeply touched me and so many others. And she always gave us something to think about later! The atmosphere in these camps was so happy that for many it was very difficult to get adjusted at home and in their jobs. What a wonderful pedagogue Tante Kees was! And it is impossible to tell how great her sense of humor was.

"She was the one who laid the foundation of faith in my heart. I always listened intensely when she was speaking. I admired her beautiful, kind, and expressive eyes, and during the campfire I looked at her simple ring with a small diamond that was sparkling so beautifully."

Corrie visited South Africa in 1953, and Pussy went to her meeting. Here was funny Tante Kees, many years and many experiences older, speaking for hundreds of people, instead of a few girls around a fire. Pussy took her husband to hear her old camp leader and said, "She so greatly impressed Henk, that he wrote to her and later was confirmed in the Dutch Reformed Church in South Africa when he was seventy-two years old."

One of Corrie's friends who played such an important role in her later life, Dr. Hans Moolenburgh of Haarlem, said, "Corrie crosses time and space." As we follow her life and influence upon so many, the significance of Dr. Moolenburgh's observation becomes sharper.

Corrie's stories were always so simplistic that it is understandable they would be remembered for scores of years. It's similar to our recollection of nursery rhymes or classic fairy tales. Her illustrations contained the wisdom of God, which finds its foundation in the verses she often quoted:

> . . . Has not God made the wisdom of this world look foolish? For it was after the world in its wisdom had failed

to know God, that he in his wisdom chose to save all who would believe by the "simple-mindedness" of the gospel message.

1 Corinthians 1:20, 21 PHILLIPS

Corrie did not instruct her camp leaders in deep theology, but she taught them to tell a story (not longer than two to five minutes) that illustrated a point. Here is a story she told me:

"There was an old monk who sang the Christmas song on Christmas Eve. His voice was very ugly, but he loved the Lord. Once the director of the cloister said, 'Now we have a new monk who has such a beautiful voice, he will sing, instead.' The man sang so beautifully that everyone was happy.

"But that night an angel came to the director of the cloister and said, 'Why didn't you have a Christmas Eve song this year?' The director said, 'What do you mean? We had such a beautiful one!' The angel said, 'But we never heard it in heaven.' "

Corrie would define her point with a simple conclusion. "Girls, the Lord hears His children who love Him, but He cannot hear the voices of those who have not accepted His Son, Jesus Christ. Does He hear your voice?"

Corrie was an organizer and a leader, but she began to see that clubs and camps needed more structure. The gymnastics club prepared the way for the beginning of the Girl Guide clubs (the European equivalent of Girl Scouts) in Holland. Corrie's girls adopted the triangle as their emblem and became known as the Triangle Girls. The triangle represented the three stages of development: social, intellectual, and physical; the circle indicated the spiritual dimension. Corrie explained, "We emphasized that when the triangle was within the circle, we were in the proper position in our lives as children of God."

Corrie raced through her middle years without regard for her age or singleness. She donned her Girl Guide uniform and walked and marched with the teenagers. She loved a joke and enjoyed making fun of herself. Father was always the picture of dignity, while Corrie remained the perennial prankster.

Every year there was a great celebration on Queen Wilhelmina's birthday, August 31. It resembled an old-fashioned American Fourth of July, with picnics, parades, and speeches. In Haarlem,

Casper ten Boom was the chairman of the parade committee and donned his best black suit and top hat, every bit the refined gentleman. For one parade, Corrie's Girl Guides marched beside an elaborate horsedrawn carriage, coachmen in uniforms guiding the matched stallions. When the official photo of this prestigious occasion was released, the girls were proper and smiling in their crisp uniforms, but Corrie had poked her head out of the resplendent carriage and made a funny face.

Corrie's light could not be hidden under a bushel. Some American women involved in YMCA work heard of her and sometime during the 1930s invited her to an international conference in Riga, Latvia. This little country, now swallowed by the communists, was then independent and had religious freedom.

At that conference Corrie was initiated into the leadership ranks of the Girl Guides from all over the world. However, there was a dimension to their activities that seemed missing. "There was a lot of talk about 'character building,'" Corrie recalled. "But the spiritual training was a disappointment."

Corrie, the newcomer, raised a pointed question, "Don't you think that we miss the purpose when we tell the girls to be good citizens, but fail to bring them to Jesus Christ?"

To her amazement, it was agreed to put an emphasis upon evangelism. When she returned to Holland, she asked some of the women she knew from her club work to help her form a national board of directors. They came from all corners of the tiny country and held their board meetings in a central place, the first-class waiting room in the Amsterdam railway station.

Many hours throughout Corrie's later life were spent meeting and planning in train stations, and later airports, throughout the world. I first met Corrie in the cocktail lounge of the United Airlines Red Carpet room. She seemed blind to the fact that the location was one she would never voluntarily frequent.

Corrie could not compromise. When she saw the erosion of Christian standards within the Girl Guide movement and the substitution of "moral instruction," there came a time when a new Christian movement was born, called *De Nederlandse Meisjesclubs* (Netherlands Girls' Clubs).

The first article of club law was: "Seek your strength through prayer." This was Corrie's motto. She used it when she was happy; she used it when she was desperate; and she passed it on to others.

In a bitter time in the future, Corrie was sitting in a dark, stone cubicle in a prison in Scheveningen, Holland, and she heard sounds of sobbing in a cell nearby. She called out, "Don't cry—be strong —we'll be free soon."

How glorious that familiar voice must have sounded! Who could mistake her voice?

"Tante Kees—is that you? I'm Annie. Oh, Tante Kees, I'm so sorry you're here, too."

Annie was one of Corrie's faithful club girls. She had been arrested by the Gestapo and taken to prison. She had never been a very brave or strong girl, as Corrie remembered. How could she help her? "Annie, do you remember the first article of our club law? 'Seek your strength through prayer.' "

What happens when a person is stripped of possessions, home, and his very freedom? Life becomes very simple, and the true essentials of existence are revealed. The children, the clubs, the Bible studies gave stamina to the lives of many who were later touched by tragedy.

Another club girl, Truus Benes, recalled, "I found Corrie was an extraordinary, tough lady, who always could find a way out when we were in difficulties. Most important, she pointed us to the work of our Great Sender. She was a pushing power in the work with the girls and stimulated us very much."

God was equipping this "tough lady" for more trials. Soon the quiet years were to be over; the clubs were closed. Corrie remembered the last time they were together. The girls sang the national anthem, struggling through their tears. She said, "Girls, don't cry. We have had great fun in our clubs, but that wasn't why we came together. Jesus makes us strong, even in times of war and disaster."

Part II

The Turning Point

When God takes one of His children and uses her in a mighty way, He chooses the one who is available. He knows her weaknesses and strengths, her talents and gifts. He also knows her breaking points.

Living in a time when the world is torn by terrorism, when leaders of nations cannot move without heavy protection and revolution stalks the earth, we wonder how we could face the suffering that could befall us at any moment. In the midst of plenty, starvation is remote; surrounded by ease and freedom, slavery is unthinkable. However, as we read of Corrie and others who are examples of unbelievable courage, we wonder: *Could I survive under such circumstances and keep my sanity?*

The turning point may be announced by the ring of a telephone or a knock on the door.

What is God saying to us through His servant, Corrie?

God used her to speak to us, about the fleeting value of things and the lasting worth of a character disciplined, molded, and strengthened by Him.

8

God Help Holland... and Us

Many Hollanders in the late 1930s were ignoring the ominous rumblings of war surrounding their beautiful country. They had been neutral before, and they would be again. However, there were some who saw the increasing threat, and among those were Queen Wilhelmina and her faithful subject Casper ten Boom.

Queen Wilhelmina wrote an accurate prediction in her autobiography: "By the spring of 1938, when Hitler invaded Austria, the answer was plain to me. German policy would result in a European catastrophe."[14]

In the lovely city of Haarlem, the chimes of St. Bavo called worshipers to church; the Grote Markt bustled with the sales of farmers and merchants, and the ten Boom watch shop, tended by Casper and his two middle-aged daughters, continued in the same daily activities that it had for years.

When the Second World War began, Holland immediately issued the usual declaration of neutrality.

However, the news came on the radio of the invasion of one country after another. In April of 1940 came the distressing report of the surprise attack on Denmark and the invasion of Norway. Like a huge weight being lowered from the top, those countries at the northernmost tip of Europe were controlled by Hitler's men.

Then it happened. Corrie and Betsie were shaken by the sound of bombs falling on Schiphol, the airport near Haarlem. To all the peaceful people who wanted to believe in their hearts, "It can't happen here," stark reality had arrived.

Corrie ran to Betsie's room, and they sat, like frightened children, with their arms around each other, and prayed.

"Lord, make us strong. Take away our fear. Give us trust."

"Betsie, God has the whole world in His hand."

"Corrie, the hairs of our head are numbered."

In Corrie's mind that night came a vision of all the family being driven away from Haarlem, in what she thought was an old-fashioned farm wagon. In many of her talks and books in later years, Corrie spoke of that dream, perhaps elaborating on the story, with the passing of time. Nevertheless, it was vivid enough to have her remember the details in years to come.

Early in the morning Corrie, Betsie, and Father gathered around the radio and listened to the serious proclamation of the Queen: "My people . . . after all these months during which our country has scrupulously observed a strict neutrality, and while its only intention was to maintain this attitude firmly and consistently, a surprise attack without the slightest warning was launched on our territory by the German armed forces last night. . . ."

Huddled around the radio, Betsie, Corrie, and Father must have gasped as the significance of the attack penetrated their secure little world.

The Queen continued in what was to be a very significant charge to all good Hollanders, "I and my government will continue to do our duty. You will do yours, everywhere and in all circumstances, each in the place he occupies, with the utmost vigilance and the inner peace and devotion which a clear conscience affords."[15]

The fear during the night and the morning of the first day of the war was the worst Corrie had ever experienced. She said that even the war, the occupation, and the destruction of their family life, just as she saw in her vision, were not as dreadful as the raw emotion of that first shock. Corrie reflected in later years, "Was it an inoculation the Lord gave to make us prepared for the future?"

Five days of war followed. It was such a short period to create such prolonged misery. The watch shop became a haven of comfort for many; Father prayed with everyone who came. Corrie frequently went to the piano to play Bach, which always gave her peace when she was troubled.

German paratroopers dropped over the Hague, and confusion in the ill-prepared Dutch army was widespread. After their first experience of battle with the enemy paratroopers, the Hollanders were hardly able to distinguish between friend and foe. The air force was too small to resist, and the German tank columns were overpowering.

The darkest day of the five-day war was when the royal family fled, Queen Wilhelmina for England and the Crown Princess Juliana for Canada. Corrie was not easily given to tears, but when she heard the Queen's voice from London, she wept openly, as did many Dutch patriots. For the Dutch people, the Queen was security. Her words over the radio were compassionate and strong: "Our heart goes out to our fellow countrymen at home, who will live through difficult times. But in the end the Netherlands will recover its entire European territory with God's help."

As Corrie went out into the streets of her beloved Haarlem, her heart aching with the misery of humiliation and defeat, she experienced a oneness in the local citizens that a common disaster can create. She thought, *In the millennium it will be like this, the whole world covered with the knowledge of God as the waters cover the bottom of the sea; one, not in misery, but one in the Lord.*

Like the beginning of a long, increasingly debilitating illness, the occupation was not unbearable at first. The watch shop buzzed with German soldiers coming in to make purchases of watches and clocks. Corrie talked to them, remembering the fresh-faced young men whom her Tante Jans had invited to her Bible studies during the First World War. But these young men were different, some of them were so brusque, so hard from childhood indoctrination in their own superiority.

As the German tanks, cavalry, and soldiers marched down the Barteljorisstraat Corrie noticed some of them seemed embarrassed and would not look at the citizens. After the war a German told her, "Every step I took in Holland, I felt ashamed. I knew I was occupying a neutral nation."

For Corrie, a forty-eight-year-old woman, the beginning of the occupation was almost exciting. The routine of the shop, the club work, and the daily walks was changed, but the new challenges were stimulating.

The Psalms, which were always central to the ten Boom's life, gained a new value during those days. Churches were packed, and ministers who never had preached about the Second Coming of

Christ were offering encouragement from the Scriptures.

But slowly the German administration began to impose restrictions. First it was in small ways, such as a curfew. It was easy in the beginning, but gradually the hours were cut back until the Dutch could not leave their houses after six o'clock. Then rationing of food began and the confiscation of cars, radios, gold, tin, copper, and even bronze church bells.

As the first cold winter of the occupation began, there came a gradual realization of the anti-Semitic measures of the German administration. In November of 1940, the Germans decreed that all Jews should be removed from government posts, schools, and universities. Many Dutch officials complied with these orders, but a few resigned. One said, "As a Christian, I cannot put myself over someone of another race." Three weeks later the Germans put him in prison.[16]

"We will continue to support the Jews," Casper said. "They are the apple of God's eye."

Most Dutch people were strongly loyal to the House of Orange, which enraged the German occupation head, Dr. Arthur Seyss-Inquart, and resulted in the elimination of all references to the Queen, or the royal house. Even street names referring to living members of the House of Orange were to be eliminated.

The years of 1941 and 1942 saw the most intense effort to remake Holland in the German image. A strong pro-Nazi organization was the *Nationaal Socialistische Bond* (or the NSB) which consisted of Dutch collaborators. German police rule became more rigid. These Dutch must be controlled! Each inhabitant over fifteen years of age had to carry an identity card. It bore the photograph, signature, and fingerprints of the owner. Jews had the letter J stamped on their cards. How important these cards became in the work of the underground resistance in the next few years. Since ration books were available only to those who reported in person and presented an identity card, it soon became obvious that J was the mark of doom.[17]

The first items to be confiscated by the Germans were bicycles. People would be riding on an errand or a visit and suddenly confront a bicycle blockade. Their means of transportation would be taken, and they were given a receipt that had no value. Some people who were allowed to keep their bicycles had the tires taken, to be sent to Germany to be melted and used for their war vehicles.

Corrie learned to ride a bicycle without tires, feeling the bumps from every cobblestone vibrate through her body as she traveled along the streets of Haarlem.

Inconvenience was soon replaced by terror when sudden disappearances of Jews or able-bodied men would grip the citizens with a constant, all-pervading fear. Soon assassinations took place as reprisals for what the Germans called acts of sabotage.

In Haarlem a German soldier was mysteriously shot, and as a result there was a Wehrmacht order requiring that a minimum of ten civilians be shot for each attack on a soldier.

The beginning of the end for the Jews in Holland came when they were forced to wear a yellow star on their clothing. Father was deeply wounded by the hatred generated for the people he loved so much.

"Corrie, will you buy a yellow star for me? I will wear one."

Corrie would not allow him to identify himself, knowing that he would be killed with the Jews. However, in his dignified, gallant manner, he took off his hat to every Jew he met.

One day Casper was visited by an old friend, the rabbi of Haarlem. Father had often prayed with him; they had read the Old Testament together and exchanged books. He came into the Beje, struggling under a mound of books, the strain of constant tension showing on his kind face. He brought back the books Father had given him and brought many of his own valued possessions, including jewelry and watches. It was the last time they ever saw him. One of his sons survived, but after the war Corrie was not able to return the treasured belongings, since the Gestapo had stolen them when the ten Booms were arrested.

For a time the Dutch sense of humor prevailed, with Hitler jokes predominating. However, when the Jews were deported, Corrie wrote, "Our misery became too deep for jokes. Another thing that happened then was that we in Holland stopped singing."

The Beje had always been a place of music, and Betsie said, "A Christian must be able to sing Psalms in the night." Corrie notified their friends that on Monday evenings there would be gospel singing in the Beje. It seemed the least they could do to keep up their spirits during those dark days.

However, there was more important work waiting for the two old-fashioned sisters and their patriarchal father.

Corrie and Betsie tried to protect Father from the increasing terror tactics of the Gestapo. Once Corrie was walking with him along the street and saw dozens of Jewish families being pushed into an old bus. "I tried to draw Father's attention to something else, but he had seen it and stopped. Father had many friends in Germany. I looked at Father's face and could not speak. I saw a sadness that I had not seen before. At last he spoke.

" 'I tremble when I think of the condemnation coming over Germany. They have touched the apple of God's eye.' "

Hitler's vision of postwar Europe was one in which the Dutch were to be a part of the Germanic union. Hitler had said that the best representatives of the Germanic race could be found in the Netherlands and in Norway. However, National Socialist doctrine claimed that the Aryan races had an implacable enemy in the Jewish race and that in order to create a pure civilization, it was the intention of the Nazi leaders to drive all Jews from positions of power in Europe, to segregate them, and eventually to remove them from the continent.

The evils of the occupation began slowly. First the cooperation with the new regime was "voluntary." The resistance was more symbolic than active.

Once Corrie's nephew Peter van Woerden, an extremely talented young musician, was the organist in a Dutch Reformed church. At the conclusion of a Sunday sermon, Peter pulled all the stops on the gigantic organ and defiantly played the "Wilhelmus," the Dutch national anthem, which was forbidden by the German authorities. Father, his old heart beating faster, was the first to his feet, singing of his love for the Queen and Holland.

Anti-German sentiment grew, as it became more obvious that German actions were becoming increasingly repressive. To many Dutch citizens, resistance became necessary in order to maintain self-respect. Dutch university students were among the first groups to encourage the growth of resistance. In 1943 fourteen thousand Dutch university students were told they could not continue their studies unless they signed a paper declaring, "I shall refrain from any act against the German Reich and the German army." Eighty-six percent of the students did not sign. Universities closed. All the people who didn't sign were summoned to the German courts on the fifth of May and were to be sent to Germany as forced labor.[18]

As in every step of life, there are choices to make. One eighteen-year-old-student, Hans Poley, was the son of a friend of Corrie's. When Hans refused to sign the loyalty oath, his mother went to the

Beje and talked to Corrie. "We cannot have Hans stay at home. It would only be a matter of time before the German police found him. Corrie, will you take Hans into your home?"

Just one small request, which was the beginning of the underground activity in that quiet little house. Corrie immediately said, "Okay, let him come."

Hans, a handsome and daring young man, moved in during the night and became a family member who remained in the house from May 9, 1943 to February 5, 1944, when he was arrested.

Corrie said, "We had not planned our rescue work. People started coming to us, saying, 'The Gestapo is behind us,' and we took them in. Soon others followed."

The ten Booms were not completely unique in their underground activities. Many brave men, women, and teenagers nursed Allied fliers who had been shot down and stashed away arms air-dropped by the Allies. One of the strongest activities of the resistance movement was hiding "underdivers," the Dutch Jews and young men who were sought by the German police.

To Corrie it was a form of relief to be able to do something. Soon her organizational talents came into use. A knock on the door, a quick look down the alley, and a young Jewish mother with her baby would slip into the Beje. She would be found a home in the country and a safe place, for a time at least.

Betsie, who was not physically strong, handled the domestic activities, and as the number of permanent and transitory guests increased she would assign duties to others. The house became like a busy office, with people coming and going, workers sent on errands, and requests being filled.

From what Corrie wrote in later years and from interviews with people who lived in the Beje during that crucial nine-month period, we can construct an image of the activities that took place. Corrie went about her business in what was called her boy-scout way, organizing, running the show. She obviously relished the new excitement in her life. Some of the young people who began to be the runners and workers were secretly amused by the ten Boom sisters, with their old-fashioned manners and ways of dressing. In the 1940s, the women wore calf-length dresses. Corrie and Betsie usually dressed in black, with dresses of indeterminate style, usually worn by women in their sixties or seventies.

Soon the Beje began to be known as the "happiest underground address in all the Netherlands." A fine violinist, a young lawyer who had been forced underground, might entertain with a Tartini sonata. Another time there would be an evening of games or a time of language study. A few of the guests turned into permanent residents, becoming a part of the family. There was a core of six to eight people who stayed, with Father and Betsie taking active parts in management. Corrie was the head of the business activity. She said, "I brought people together." And what a diverse number of people and needs! The Beje Gang consisted of a group of thirty boys and twenty girls in addition to twenty older men and ten women. They were organized, dispatched, and directed by Corrie.

Problems piled up each day. A Jewish woman was about to have a baby; a doctor and a hospital must be found. A historical account of that time told about the outstanding example of the medical profession in its refusal to assist the Germans in their war effort. Then there were the people who became ill or the ones who died. How could a Jew be buried without endangering other members of his family or those who were assisting him? One resistance worker told of putting a dead woman in a wheelchair and going to an Amsterdam canal. "In peacetime I would have walked arm in arm with my boyfriend along that canal, but now I watched a little Jewish grandmother disappear in the dark water."[19]

Corrie's little bedroom became a clearinghouse for supply and demand: a place for a child; twenty more ration cards; someone to go to a shed on the public tennis courts, where a man was lying seriously ill. Corrie was the matriarchal dispatcher, encouraging her team into action. "All right, boys, let's get busy. Who will arrange for transportation? Who for an address?" Subterfuge, which had never been a part of Corrie's personality, became a survival trait.

Refugees came and went in the Beje, but one small nucleus always remained. Meyer Mossel (whose nickname was Eusie), Mary, and Thea were the Jews; Peter and Hans, students; and Leendert, a teacher. Soon it became evident that there should be a hiding place where the underdivers could go if and when the Gestapo ever invaded their house. A secret room was built with access under the bottom shelf of Corrie's closet. It would hold approximately eight people. On the floor was a mattress, a supply of Victoria water (a soft drink), and some Sanovit (health biscuits). It was called the Angelcrib.

It was a time of tension, but also a time of joy. Corrie told how their love for the Jews increased while they shared danger. Once they had a Hanukkah feast; Father brought out a Hanukkah lamp they had in the shop, and their guests were delighted. Eusie, a cantor of the synagogue, one of the more permanent guests, added to the celebration by singing in his full, rich baritone.

A neighbor who lived opposite the Beje came over and said, "Could you tell your Jews to close the curtains when they celebrate their feasts? I have followed with great interest what they have been doing during the last hour, but not all your neighbors are safe. One traitor who sees a glimpse of your enthusiastic guests could bring all of you to a concentration camp."

Every night before retiring, all of the guests-in-transit would take their outer and underclothing into the Angelcrib. Eusie's suspenders would trail behind him as he carried in his clothes, which amused Corrie. It was a tragicomedy atmosphere in the Beje. For a while the drills were like games. Rewards of cream puffs (made with very little precious sugar) were given for good performances. Corrie would press an alarm bell, pull out her stopwatch, and see how fast everyone could disappear into the hiding place. They would duck down and vanish under the shelf, with legs folded in last. Then the boxes and laundry would be replaced on the floor of the closet and the sliding door closed.

"Just seventy seconds that time. Good." Corrie would then make the rounds of the rooms, to see if any remnants of the inhabitants were left. Eusie dropped some cigar ashes, Hans forgot a collar stud. From the closet Corrie heard Eusie's very Jewish voice say, "Mary, you're blowing in my neck!" Mary was asthmatic, and her heavy breathing threatened their safety.

Corrie tried to stay insulated from the suffering and cruelty she knew were being brought on the Jews. Once Mary suddenly threw her arms around Corrie and sobbed, "My people, my people, how we have to suffer!" Corrie held her close and couldn't speak. Words would have seemed empty. Here was an ocean of suffering and cruelty poured out on God's ancient people. It was almost danger-ous to realize the situation, for it could break your heart. She had to be strong for the underground activities.

Corrie prayed, "Father, in Jesus' Name, have mercy upon your people. Lord, help us bring liberation. Let this terrible war end soon."

Corrie did not attempt to "evangelize" or convert the Jews who came to their home. Hans Poley, the student who became a busi-nessman after the war, said, "The ten Booms were very outgoing

Christians, but they did not attempt to convert. The Jews who came into the house were persecuted, so their attitude was very defensive."

In later times, however, the prayers and Bible reading of Father, who was affectionately called *Opa*, "Grandfather," by all, were echoed by some of their Jewish friends. Mary was taken prisoner and told one of Corrie's former club girls, "I listened to what Opa said about Jesus, and I believed he was right. I believe Jesus is my Messiah and have asked Him to enter my heart."

It was at that moment that her cell door was opened, and Mary was called out. She was not heard of again.

Fear was an overriding emotion among the Beje transients and guests. But Eusie said, "Here in our Beje nothing can happen. There are angels around us. I have never seen a house like this. If there is need for anything, the people pray, and it comes—often immediately."

The outreach was not only to the hunted, but also the hunters. Corrie told how once a German soldier came into the shop and, seeing that she was alone, said, *"Grüss Gott,"*

"Why don't you say, *'Heil Hitler'?"* she asked.

"I don't believe in Hitler, I believe in God."

Never one to hesitate in determining someone's true standing, Corrie asked, "Do you believe in Jesus Christ?"

When the young soldier told her he was a Christian, she invited him to come to a Bible meeting the next night. The following evening all the Jews were safely hidden, the house cleaned of all papers that could show that more than the little family of three occupied the premises, and some hymn books borrowed from a German church. But nobody came.

Two days later Corrie met the boy in the street. He said that he was going to Germany on furlough for two weeks, but would organize a real Bible study when he returned. He never had his furlough; things were going badly for the German army in Russia, and all furloughs were canceled. Corrie saw that as a sign from the Lord that the young man should study with them. "Can we have a meeting tonight then?" she asked.

"No, we shouldn't. In my hometown a friend had an organized Bible meeting with soldiers. The Gestapo came and sent the father of the family to one prison, the mother to another, and the children to a third one. These were Germans, Miss ten Boom. What do you think the Gestapo would do with a Dutch family who does the same?"

Father was listening to this conversation. He brought the German soldier into the workshop, laid his hand on his shoulder, and prayed. Casper ten Boom did not hate the German occupying forces, he pitied them. Perhaps it was the shield his family placed around him to guard him from the increasing Gestapo atrocities, or maybe it was his own intrinsic love for all men.

In 1943 Allied victories were becoming more frequent, and the German police in Holland were inflicting increasingly severe reprisals on the Dutch. A Hollander, remembering the prevailing fear of those days said, "We never knew who would be shot or when. If someone was taken to prison, he might be pulled from his cell and lined up before a firing squad."

In the spring of 1943, the underground workers and "guests" in the Beje listened to the angry words of Queen Wilhelmina, broadcasting from London and secretly heard by concealed radios in the homes of Dutch patriots. "I want to raise a fiery protest against the cunningly organized and constantly extended manhunt which the German hordes, assisted by national traitors, are carrying out all over the country.

"Our language lacks the words to describe these infamous practices."[20]

Some of the Beje Gang thought that Corrie and Betsie and their "guardian angels" were foolish illusions of two old maids. However, the day arrived when it seemed that the angels broke ranks.

9

On the Front Line

Nollie was arrested by the Gestapo!

Corrie jumped on her bike, with its bent rims, and bumped to her sister's house, about a mile and a half from the Beje. She was careful not to stop when she saw the Gestapo inside, searching. Was this to be the beginning of the end of their hiding the Jews and others in need of protection?

As if to answer her unspoken question, Corrie heard the familiar strains of Bach's beautiful hymn, "Jesu, Joy of Man's Desiring," coming from Nollie's house, even while the German police hunted for incriminating evidence. Nollie's son Fred, a theological student, was playing the piano. He had not been arrested, because he told the Gestapo that he was an assistant minister in a small church. Sometimes the Germans had respect for the clergy. The youngest son, Peter, had escaped over the roof of the house.

The Germans had found two Jews in Nollie's house, and consequently, she was arrested. Corrie listened to the heavenly Bach music and prayed, "Lord, thank You for reminding me that You have Nollie's life in Your hands and that You are the source of her joy."

There was no time to waste in staring at Nollie's house, so Corrie raced home and told all the underdivers they must leave at once. For a short period of time the activities at the Beje ceased, until they were sure the Gestapo was not going to search another ten Boom home.

To know that Nollie was in prison was a terrible reality that shocked Corrie and Betsie and weakened Father. When they were little girls, Corrie had run to Nollie for comfort. Now Corrie's *moedertje* was in prison. Where would these terrible actions against the innocent lead?

Corrie knew she would do anything to have Nollie released; when Corrie decided, she was undaunted by human obstacles. Nollie would be free. No prison would hold one of her loved ones!

Nollie was brought to the police station first, where her cell was filthy and during the night mice ran over her dirty blanket. Corrie knew that the mother of one of the young Dutch students she had aided in hiding from the Germans was working in the police station. This woman became the contact point for information about Nollie.

One morning Corrie was told that Nollie was being sent by transport to another prison. Corrie maintained a vigil at the gate of the police station and after many hours of waiting saw her sister between two policemen, being marched through the doors. Corrie ignored the men and threw her arms around her. Nollie smiled and said, "God is love!"

Corrie was shaken. How could Nollie be so calm? Corrie could have understood if she had said, "Can you believe that God would allow the enemy to bring me to prison?" But, no, Nollie had given her experience wings: one wing, surrender; the other wing, trust.

This gentle Dutch mother was shoved into the prison van, where it was very dark and she could barely stand in a tight cubicle. Suddenly there was a beam of light through a hole in the door, and she took a pencil she had hidden in her thick hair and wrote on the wall, "Jesus is Victor."

Nollie was a constant source of strength to her prison mates. She was put in a completely darkened cell with another woman, who was sobbing in the corner.

"Cheer up," Nollie said to her. "We won't stay here forever."

"Don't you cry?" the woman asked. "We all cry when we come here for the first time."

"Why should I cry? God never makes mistakes, even when He allowed the enemy to bring me here."

Corrie began her rounds to have Nollie released. She went to

Gestapo officers, police stations, and visited other underground organizations. She was scolded, laughed at, and thrown out of offices, but she never gave up. Finally, there was a little beam of hope. She heard that the German doctor who was in charge of sick prisoners in the area was said to be a compassionate man. At that time Corrie was reading Dale Carnegie's book *How to Win Friends and Influence People*. One of the principles she applied was to find out about a person's hobby and talk about it.

She went to the doctor's house and boldly asked to see him, not knowing what she would encounter. At home, people were praying for Corrie's venture and for God's wisdom for her.

Upon entering the doctor's home, she saw three large dogs, and the Carnegie technique was quickly used. The doctor came to meet her, and after respectfully greeting him, Corrie said, "You have such beautiful dogs. What is the breed?"

The doctor became quite animated and began to tell her about his pets and what wonderful companions they were when he was separated from his family. Finally he stopped, looked at this Dutch woman of an indeterminate age, and said, "I am sure you did not come to talk about dogs. What is it you want?"

Corrie became very direct. "My sister, Nollie van Woerden, is in prison. She is not well, and I'm sure prison life could be fatal. Her only crime is that she had two Jews in her house."

The doctor looked at the prison roll and said, "There is no one here of that name."

It was then that Corrie found out for the first time that women prisoners went by their maiden names. It was a minor item, but just another psychological method of diminishing dignity.

The doctor looked up *ten Boom* and said, "Oh, yes, I know her. She is certainly ill. However, don't worry, she is not too bad, and she is a great source of cheerfulness to her fellow prisoners."

"I know that Nollie will not lose courage," Corrie said with relief. "She knows the Lord Jesus and surrenders all her problems to Him. I came to you because I believe you can help me get her out of prison."

"So, your interest is not really in dogs," the doctor teased her. "I'll do my best."

What good news Corrie had to tell at home! But a week passed, and nothing happened. Corrie went back to the doctor's house, more boldly this time, and asked him, "How are your dogs?"

"Miss ten Boom, you do not seem to trust me that I am willing to help your sister. Please leave it to me."

Corrie was on safer ground now, so she said, in her irrepressible, roguish manner, "If she is not with us within a week, I will come again to ask about your dogs."

The next day Nollie came home. Corrie knew that God had answered their prayers for release and gave her some Dale Carnegie techniques just at the right time.

During Nollie's imprisonment, there was a lull in the underground work at the Beje. After her release, the momentum of activities began to increase. Corrie returned to providing the ration and travel cards, arranging for transportation and other hiding places as the intensity of Jewish persecution and police terrorism increased.

We are told by Dutch historians who carefully studied and analyzed the Dutch under German occupation between 1940 and 1945 that the number of persons who gave up their normal way of life for full-time underground work was very small. Many Dutchmen were willing to take minor risks, but the bulk of the population, as elsewhere in occupied Western Europe, did not participate in resistance activities. It was estimated that fewer than twelve hundred patriots gave their entire time to underground activities.[21]

The danger increased every day as the ten Boom household became more obvious. One day a man who worked in the national underground movement came to Corrie and said, "You are in such danger that I must know: Can you shoot? We will give you a revolver, and whenever you are attacked, you can defend yourself. Tonight we will come for you and take you to a house far outside Haarlem, where we will give you your first shooting lessons."

Corrie told him, "I have watchmaker's hands. They are very steady. I think I am able to shoot, but I don't like this idea."

"We will come tonight. Think it over."

Corrie went to her room to pray over this hard decision. "I know, Lord, that I am in the front line of a war. But, please, Lord, let my work be to save lives, not to take lives. I will never judge what others should do, but make it clear what is Your will for me."

When the men came to take her for her shooting lesson, she said, "I won't come. I don't know what is God's will for others, but I know what God's will is for me."

The pressures began to build. Once Corrie was summoned to appear before the chief of police. She was surprised at the summons, since she thought that she could be arrested at any time. The summons seemed very mild. The family gathered, Corrie gave what she thought would be the last orders to her gang, and she surrendered her life into the hands of the Lord.

The police officer turned out to be a patriotic Dutchman who had cooperated with underground workers. He wanted her help. Knowing Corrie had underground connections all over Holland, he told her that he knew of an underground worker who was working in secret with the Germans. Since there was no "secret prison" for collaborators, he said to Corrie, "The only way to stop his devilish work is to kill him. I cannot do it, since those of us in the police are under strict control. Can you take on this project personally?"

Corrie was astounded that anyone would think that a Sunday-school teacher and youth worker could actually murder someone, no matter what evil he was performing against his fellow Dutchmen.

"No, Miss ten Boom, not you, personally, but can you find someone to whom you can give orders?"

"Are you a Christian?"

"Yes, I am."

"We'll pray."

Corrie's decisions, large and small, were always made with prayer. "Lord, touch the heart of this man and change him from a betrayer to a real Christian. Save him for eternity, Lord, and make him a tool in your hand, instead of the hand of the enemy."

God answered that prayer of Corrie's because the man targeted for assassination was converted and became a dedicated underground worker.

Corrie said that three times she had the same experience of being asked to provide a political assassin. Every time she asked for the conversion, instead of the death of the Dutch betrayer. Sometimes these people did not change, and Corrie struggled with the thought that she might have been guilty of the harm they did, because she was not willing to kill or order killings.

Corrie was frequently burdened by the secrecy, the false identification cards, assumed names, and the lies. Often she cried to the Lord about it. She examined the Old Testament to find the stories where people were in the same situation and lied and to see the way God blessed. Rahab, for instance, the harlot of Jericho, because she hid spies. The midwives in Egypt were blessed because of the lie that the Jewish mothers had given birth before they arrived.

"But Betsie, there is no place in the New Testament where we can find an excuse for lying."

In later years people said, perhaps somewhat sanctimoniously, "I could never have been able to lie as you did." Corrie would remember how she lied when the Gestapo demanded, "Where is your secret room?" Six people would have been killed if she had told the truth. When she was questioned by the judge about her underground activities she prayed, "Lord, set a watch before my mouth; guard the door of my lips." Corrie, schooled as she was in the Psalms, knew the passage well. What she admitted praying, however, was, "Lord, help me lie."

How did Corrie reconcile her lies with her solid Christian commitment? She said, "What did I do? I just brought it to the Lord and asked forgiveness. Jesus loves sinners. Love covers a multitude of sins, and love is what brought us to do our utmost to save as many people as we could."

They learned during those tension-filled times not to ask too many questions. Corrie's nephew, Kik, was an active underground worker, a member of the national movement. He was in close contact with the English army and helped parachutists by hiding them in a cabin he had built in the woods behind his house.

Once Kik and Corrie were sitting on the narrow, winding staircase in the Beje, since all the rooms in the house were occupied and it was the only place where they could talk. The doorbell rang, and Kik stiffened. Corrie felt the shock going through the young man's body and said, "Why are you afraid, Kik?"

So many of the young people thought Corrie and Betsie were unconcerned about their own safety. He said, "Tante Corrie, you are in far greater danger than you realize."

"Kik, don't you believe that the Lord will protect us with His angels? Even if He should allow us to be found, aren't we saving God's ancient people, the Jews? Listen, boy, are you a child of God?"

"Sometimes yes, sometimes no," Kik answered.

"Kik, that is impossible. When you are my brother Willem's son, you are always his son, even when you are naughty."

"That's what I am, Tante Corrie, a naughty child of God."

"Then repent, Kik, and bring your sins to Jesus."

That was the last talk Corrie had with Kik. He was arrested by the Gestapo, and for seven years after the war no one knew what had happened to him. Uncertainty during times of war and imprisonment was worse than knowing. The family finally heard that the German concentration camp where Kik was taken was liberated by the Russians, but no one was freed. They were all transported to a labor camp in Russia, where Kik died from abuse and starvation. A boy who escaped from Russia brought this news to the family.

The waiting, the uncertainties, were some of the worst consequences of war and occupation. Corrie experienced in later years the results of these anxiety experiences in Germany, where she often talked with people who went to fortune-tellers to try to find out what had happened to their loved ones. In counseling those people after the war, she heard so many of them who told about the impossibility of praying, thoughts of suicide, and other dark experiences when they came in contact with demons.

Out of her knowledge of God's Word and from personal experiences Corrie ten Boom was prepared to be on the front line of the battle.

10

Betrayed by Man

Holland in February can be very damp and cold. The wind blows in from the North Sea, bringing the penetrating chill that causes even the most robust Dutchman to wrap his heavy scarf closer around his neck. On the morning of February 28, 1944 Corrie pulled the blankets closer to comfort her aching chest and muscles. Her body was weak with fever and her throat raw from coughing. Somehow she got dressed and went downstairs, just to oversee the work for the day. She would rest later, when she knew all the details of the daily underground activities were properly assigned.

On that dreary morning, a man appeared at the door and asked to see Corrie. This wasn't an uncommon occurrence, but this man was unknown, uneasy, and wary. But then, everyone was suspicious in those days. One had to discern between a "good" Dutchman and a dangerous one. Cautiously, he said, "Miss ten Boom, my wife was arrested in Alkmaar. She had been helping many Jews. If people tell on her, her life will not be worth a penny."

Corrie listened to his story, through the fog and her fever. "We have found a policeman who will set her free if we pay him six hundred guilders. I have no money. Will you help us?"

Money was not important during those tense days. There was very little to buy—except time and lives. Corrie called her team of young people together and said, "Listen, within one hour I must have four hundred guilders. Do your best."

Corrie stumbled upstairs and, pulling off her dress, collapsed on the bed. She prayed that God would bless the money and save the life of this man's wife. How comforting the hiss of the vaporizer must have been as she drifted into a restless sleep.

For months all of the permanent and transient occupants of the Beje had been practicing their escape and cover-up routines. The drills had been so thorough that it took only seventy seconds for the rooms to look uninhabited.

When the actual alarm came, the Beje was crowded. It was on Monday afternoon. Willem was leading a Bible study; Nollie had come to visit Father; Peter, her son, was practicing on the family organ. Betsie had just finished the kitchen work, aided by several of the underdivers. No one suspected that the Dutchman who had requested money for his wife was a quisling, working secretly with the Germans. The Gestapo had ordered him to find out if Corrie ten Boom was an underground worker, and when he returned to the Beje to pick up the 600 guilders, he had his evidence.

Within five minutes of his pocketing the money, the Gestapo was at the door. The dreaded moment had come. This was not a drill, and the reward was not cream puffs, but prison and death.

Four Jewish refugees and two underground workers who were in the Beje when the alarm was sounded raced up the stairs, past Corrie's bed, and dove into the hiding place. Corrie stumbled out of bed, threw her briefcase of records in the opening, and closed the closet door. She had just fallen into bed and pulled up the covers when she heard heavy, ominous footsteps on the stairs. A surly-looking man burst into her room and shouted, "Get up, give me your identification card."

Modest Corrie, with her old-world manners, experienced the beginning of personal humiliation as she was forced to stand in her slip and fumble for her identification card in front of a sneering soldier.

"Where is your secret room?" the Gestapo agent demanded.

When Corrie refused to answer, he snapped. "Never mind. I know Jews are hidden here. We'll have the house watched until they've turned into mummies."

The Beje had become a Gestapo trap. Everyone who entered, including customers and underground workers who had seen the all-safe sign in the window (an advertisement for Alpina watches), was arrested.

Corrie was ordered downstairs and told to take off her glasses.

Father was very calm. He sat in his chair beside the fire, with an expression of complete peace on his face. Betsie came in, the welts beginning to form on her soft face, and pointed to a simple plaque over the fireplace, which read, "Jesus is Victor." Father followed the direction of her glance and said, "Yes, indeed, that is absolutely true."

There seemed to be a visible relaxation in many faces. Suddenly one of the Gestapo said to Father, "I see a Bible over there. Tell me, what does it say about the government?"

Father answered, " 'Fear God, honor the Queen.' Actually, it says, 'honor the King,' but in our case, that is the Queen."

While the Gestapo interrogation was going on downstairs, what was happening in the Angelscrib, or hiding place? Six men and women were cramped in that closet, where they were to stay for almost three days.

A missing thread in the story of this tense time has been an account of these refugees. For a vital link in this biography, one of the most exciting discoveries was finding the "official document about what happened in the Beje," written by one of the survivors. Here is a translation of chilling excerpts from this astounding document:

> In almost every town there was a good hiding place that saved underground workers or people in hiding from being arrested. One of the most important of the contacts of the LO (which was the national organization which gave assistance to "underdivers" or *onderduikers*—literally "people who go underwater") in Haarlem was the so-called Beje group in the Barteljorisstraat . . . the house got the name the Hider's Paradise. Oftentimes, one found the cream of the "illegal top" together. The family was somewhat reckless because they were convinced that the house was being protected by angels.
>
> On the 28th of February, 1944, came the blow. . . . there were three hiding places in the house. The good hiding place (the so-called upper gallery), was built in a bedroom and covered a complete wall. The length was about two

meters, the width about seventy centimeters, while the height was about two and a half to three meters. The entrance was in a closet standing in front of it and was closed off by a large trapdoor. By way of an air vent there was ventilation in this area. Just before the Gestapo entered, six people hid in there. They were: Aunt Mary and Aunt Martha (two Jewesses), Eusie and Ronni (Jews), Hans and Arnold. The door had just closed when quick footsteps and shouting voices revealed the arrival of intruders in the bedroom, where Corrie, the family daughter, was in bed, very sick. The men treated her in a scandalous way and just pulled her out of bed. After searching the room quickly, they left again, taking Corrie.

The writer of the document, obviously one of the occupants of the hiding place, then described the activities taking place downstairs. After many more unsuspecting people were lured into the Beje because of the "safe" sign in the window, the house was finally evacuated, and everyone was taken to the police station on the Smedestraat.

However, what happened to the people hiding in the upper gallery? Naturally, they had heard everything: the bells, the searching of the house, and finally the departure of the whole group. A guard, however, stayed behind, so absolute silence was essential.

The underdiver's diary continued:

Some noise was unavoidable. One had to be able to move occasionally (taking turns, four could sit down and two had to stand). Ronni had problems coughing. This noise was being smothered in a blanket . . . often it seemed as if the guard, right after one of those unavoidable noises, would come upstairs. In anxious tension one waited then, with back against the wall, so possible knocking would not sound hollow.

It got dark, and the clock on the Grote Markt chimed away the hours. Hunger set in, but there was very little food. Sleeping was impossible. At two o'clock, the changing of the guard brought some relief. After their placement in the house, they usually went around looking for something to their liking. At a certain moment one move made a lot of noise, and two men came upstairs into the room. All walls were being knocked, and the closet, the entrance to the hiding place, was being searched. They started to break planks of wood from the floor. This was seemingly a lot of work, because the men thought it was time to rest and light up one of Grandpa's cigars. Further searching was ceased after this.

Tuesday morning the situation became almost intolerable. The hunger was not the worst part. It seemed as if the stomach asked for food less and less the more time passed. But, the nerve-racking waiting . . . that was bad. Besides, the air became almost unbearable. In the corner of the hiding place there was a cookie jar in which, if absolutely necessary, one could defecate. In the same corner they had put the sheet, which had been ripped into pieces, and the blanket on which we could urinate. Because of the limited room, turns had to be taken in the "stink corner."

When, at a certain moment, on top of it all, the cookie jar was knocked over, it really became unbearable. At that moment all the conditions were present to drive somebody crazy in a short period of time. They were at the end of their rope and discussed their chances to break out. The Jews were familiar with the house and surroundings and made up a plan. It included a jump of two and one-half meters. Arnold resisted this plan; help must be on its way. Why should they take this risk? He succeeded in calming everybody somewhat, and in making them wait a little while longer. No matter how critical the situation was and which problems occurred, one thing the Jew, Eusie, knew was which way was east. Every time he prayed, and he did this many times, he always knew to turn in such a way that he was facing the east.

When 4:30 Wednesday afternoon arrived, somebody came upstairs and into the room. The closet door opened, and a tap was heard: . . .— . . . — . . . —. The V sign.

Betrayal? Help? Then a voice: "Arnold, answer." Quickly they deliberated. Win or lose, Arnold answered. The door was opened, and the faces of two policemen appeared. Quickly, however, they pulled back from the terrible smell that came out. However, their faces were recognized and trusted. Freedom was nearby. They agreed that first Arnold and Hans would be taken to the house next door, by way of a window in the roof. Then, when it was dark, the Jews would be taken away. Everything had to happen very cautiously, because there were still enemy guards downstairs.

And that's the way it happened. Arnold and Hans safely reached the street via the house next door . . . when it was dark, they succeeded in freeing the four Jews.

Arnold, the writer of this vivid account, escaped to write the story.

What happened to the ten Booms? For more than fifty years they had been honored citizens of Haarlem; now they were taken to the police station, like dangerous criminals, under armed guard. A total of thirty-five prisoners were arrested in the Beje that day, including all of Casper ten Boom's children and one grandson.

Everyone was forced to sleep on gymnastic mats and deprived of all possessions except the clothes they were wearing. Peter van Woerden, Nollie's son, recalled, "The atmosphere at the station in that big room was one of being defeated, downhearted, and betrayed. I remember how Grandfather had been praying that there would be a watch of angels around the house, and the question in my mind was, 'What happened to the angels?' "

A policeman was left to guard them, and he seemed to look at Father with compassionate eyes. He must have listened as Father read, as he did every night with his family, from the Bible. He chose Psalm 91, with its promise of security for the child of God. "You will not be afraid of the terror by night . . ." (Psalms 91:5).

Corrie asked the policeman, "Is Father the oldest prisoner you have ever had?" He avoided her question by answering, "Things are bad enough." However, he left the ten Boom family to themselves, so that they had a chance to plan together what answers they would give when they were brought to trial.

Peter remembered that long, sleepless night when he took all the incriminating papers they had on them—the addresses of underground workers and identity papers—and attempted to flush them down the toilet. Cruelty surrounded them. One Jew was brought in and beaten over and over. He held his hand on his wallet and shouted, "You can take anything, but don't take my money." The officer spit at him and said, "Don't you know you're

going to be killed? Money won't be any good to you." The guards
took him into another room, and the other prisoners heard the
beatings. He came out, blood streaming from his face, but still
holding onto his wallet.

Father seemed oblivious to his harsh surroundings. He appeared
to be living within the shelter of the Psalm that says, "A thousand
may fall at your side, And ten thousand at your right hand; But it
shall not approach you" (Psalms 91:7).

At noon the following day a bus stopped at the station, and
everyone was loaded onto it. People stood quietly, solemnly, with
tears in their eyes as Haarlem's Grand Old Man and his family were
pushed roughly up the steps. Corrie, trying to reassure Father, said,
"Just think, when we see Haarlem next, it will be free."

Betsie who seemed to have some gifted insight, answered, "No,
Corrie, you will see it before then."

Corrie, remembering that day, said, "In my heart was a great
sense of peace. I had long expected this catastrophe. Now the blow
had fallen. I accepted it as the close of an exciting chapter of my life.
In my mind I kept telling myself, "Don't ever feel sorry for yourself."

Where were they being taken? The sleepless night and the shock
of the raid left the family and their underground co-workers in
numb shock as the bus labored south, toward the seaside town of
Scheveningen, which in happier days, was a lovely resort area. In
spite of the uncertainty of their destination, there was a certain
security in being together as a family.

When they arrived at the Bureau of the Gestapo, the questioning
began. Endless questions, accusations, and repetitions continued all
day. Father grew very weak and confused. Finally one of the inter-
rogators said, "You might as well let that man die at home." However, the captain who had arrested them in the Beje shouted, "That
man is the worst of them all. He talks about nothing but Jesus and
the Queen."

What a distortion of morality was programmed into the minds of
those young Germans, who were trained to hate the weak, the old,
and imperfect; and cruelty, in the name of the Reich, was justified!
Corrie wrote in a book, which was sold by the thousands in postwar
Germany, that when she stood in the Gestapo interrogation center,
she began to despair. Perhaps she was on the edge of shock, racked
with a bronchial cough and hot with fever. She wrote:

My whole body started to tremble. Suddenly I saw Peter, Nollie's youngest son. There was an expression of peace on his face. He seemed to be talking with the Lord. It was the third time he had been in prison. The first time the Lord had put His hand on Peter's life, and he came back from prison a changed boy, determined to become an evangelist-musician.

"I am with you always," Jesus had said. Through Peter's face I realized the presence of the Lord—a security that could not be damaged.

From the Gestapo headquarters the family was loaded into a decrepit vehicle without springs or seats and transported to the great prison of Scheveningen. It reminded Corrie of the carts that carried prisoners to the guillotine during the French Revolution. Or was it like the old farm wagon she had seen in a dream, on the night when bombs first shook Holland? Somehow, in some mysterious way, this terrible trip was just the way she had envisioned it.

At the first in a series of three prisons, Corrie was separated from her family. As she saw her sisters, brother, and nephew disappear into the dank corridors, with the sound of the steel doors clanking behind them, the bleakness of this nightmarish situation began. But it was hardest of all to be separated from Father, who had an expression of tranquility on his noble face. As he was ushered to his cell, Corrie kissed him and whispered, "The Lord be with you." He answered, softly, "And with you, my daughter."

That was the last time she saw Father on earth. He lived for ten days after his arrest and died in a hospital corridor. It was almost two months before Corrie knew what happened to him.

Betsie may have anticipated the type of death this saintly old man of God would have. She wrote from cell 314:

So our dear father has now been promoted to Glory. And how? The Lord Himself crowned his head with the martyr's crown. Many years ago I had a premonition of this, but I steadfastly put it out of my mind. I often thought that a person in whom Christ was shown to such full advantage, who lived so close to the Savior, to whom the eternal things were so real, and who had the gift of prayer in such a wonderful way—such a person has all the conditions for

becoming a martyr. And then I thought, "He is not going
to die in his bed." All this only came back to mind after he
had died. . . . Just before his death the Lord took him away
from his dear ones in order to be able to give him the crown
of honor. God did not let His Sovereignty slip from His
fingers.

For the first ten days in prison, Corrie was in a cell with five other
prisoners. The cell was deep and narrow, scarcely any wider than
the metal door. One small cot was crammed against the wall, and
filthy straw mattresses on the floor were beds for the other prisoners.

As Corrie entered the cell, she shook with an uncontrollable
spasm of coughing. The other women pressed their backs against
the wall to avoid her. Whether out of kindness or fear of infec-
tion, she was given the cot and sank gratefully onto it, only to
have her first indication of what inhuman living would be like.
Vomit and urine combined odors in the straw pallet to add to the
misery.

Those first few days were spent in trying to show some sort of
kindness to her cellmates, but soon Corrie became too ill to do
anything but toss on the thin pallet, with her head throbbing and
her arms shot with pain. In her feverish, weakened condition, she
worried most about Father. Betsie and she had always cared for him
so tenderly. She remembered praying, "O Lord, take him home to
Thee in heaven. It will be so good for him!"

During her second week of imprisonment, Corrie was suddenly
ordered to get dressed and come outside. She was told she was being
taken to the consultation bureau. She rode through the streets of the
Hague in a beautiful car, wondering how people could be walking
the streets, streetcars could be running, and the sun could shine. The
ordinary activities were so unnatural.

At the consultation bureau, Corrie asked if she could go to the
bathroom. A nurse accompanied her, and when the door was closed,
impulsively put her arms around Corrie and said, "Can I help you
in any way?"

In the midst of hell, a touch of human kindness! From this
friendly nurse she received some essential toilet items such as a
toothbrush and soap and a great treasure, copies of the four Gospels!

The doctor diagnosed that she had pleurisy and thought that she might get tuberculosis. "You could infect fellow prisoners," he said. "Therefore, we will put you alone in a cell."

Empty. Gray. Cell 384. Corrie had never been alone for any length of time in her entire life. A storm swirled outside, and she was chilled to the bone.

"O Savior, You are with me. Help me; hold me fast and comfort me," she prayed.

In the first few weeks, she was desperately sick and lonely. In the beginning, her bread was thrown to her, like scraps to a caged, infected animal.

One day the *Sanitäter* (orderly or Red Cross worker) brought her some medicine. Desperately anxious for news, she asked him, "Is my father still living?"

"I don't know," he replied. "And if I did I wouldn't be permitted to tell you."

A few minutes later the *Wachtmeisterin* (female head guard) stormed into Corrie's cell and shouted, "If you ever dare to ask the Sanitäter about another prisoner, you will not receive any medical attention at all."

Corrie had greeted the Wachtmeisterin with a pleasant, "Good morning," and was answered with an armor of hate. Was there no love left in the world?

When she grew stronger, Corrie filled her time with invented activities: She made friends with some ants and began to talk with them and feed them bread crumbs. Once, when she was cleaning the floor, she accidentally touched some of the ants with her rag, and they ran and hid in their little hole.

She thought of the words from Psalm 91 that Father had read in the police station: "The Lord is your refuge." Sometimes she wondered how the Lord could help her in such a hopeless situation as being in prison, dirty and desolate, not knowing about her family and friends, and reduced to conversing with ants. She wrote this: "I looked at the last ant. I am sure it did not look at its little legs or around at the rag that had threatened it. It looked straight into the hole in the wall. That was its refuge. I prayed, 'Lord Jesus, You are my refuge, I'll just look at You.'"

When deprived of everything except life itself, some people go mad or become filled with hatred; others find meaning out of suffering. Viktor Frankl, author-psychiatrist, who survived three years in the infamous Auschwitz concentration camp, wrote, "In the concentration camp every circumstance conspires to make the prisoner lose his hold. All the familiar goals in life are snatched away. What alone remains is the last of human freedoms—the ability to choose one's attitude in a given set of circumstances."[22]

In solitary confinement, Corrie ten Boom thought of the poetic triplet that she later repeated hundreds of times throughout the world:

> Look around and be distressed.
> Look inside and be depressed.
> Look at Jesus and be at rest.

For mental health, boredom must be replaced with activity. Corrie had a stay out of her corset that she sharpened on the floor and used as a knife. Painstakingly, she dug away at a little hole between two bricks. One day, she reached her glorious goal! She had a hole large enough to be able to talk with five women in the cell next to hers. One girl in particular talked about the Lord, so Corrie whispered, "Listen, give me a text you know by heart. You and I will both meditate upon the words and try to make a sermon. Tonight you tell me your sermon, and I will tell you mine."

They shared their mini-sermons and optimistic thoughts about liberation. Later this girl was beaten and died in Ravensbruck.

During four months of solitary, Corrie was allowed outside in the prison yard only once. She had a brief reunion with Annie, one of her club girls, which gave a great lift to her spirits. Annie whispered, "Tante Kees, pray for me, and I'll pray for you." Corrie later heard that Annie had been released and that she was a great source of encouragement to her cell mates.

"What a miracle Jesus can perform in a weak girl who seeks her strength in prayer, and what a strong guide Jesus is when even the weakest hand is laid on His strong one," Corrie wrote about Annie.

A week after Corrie celebrated a grim, solitary birthday, the letter came from Nollie: "Darling, now I have to tell you something very sad. Be strong. On the tenth of March, our dear father went to heaven."

Corrie knew that she would see her beloved father again in Glory, but the present was so empty—a world so cruel, so insecure. He was a kind of rock in the midst of the stormy life.

It was then she prayed, "Father, in Jesus' Name, let me show that love I cannot give to him anymore, to other people who will need it."

The touch with the outside world, through Nollie's letter, made Corrie more lonely than before. But then the Scripture came to her, "The suffering of this time is not worthy to be compared with the coming glory."

It was as if Father had said it. A feeling of rest and comfort came into her heart.

The weeks and months stretched out interminably. One day Corrie was stretched on her cot, a dirty, smelly blanket covering her to her waist, her bare arms thin and mottled from malnutrition and cold. Her nails, once so clipped and clean to handle fine watch parts, were long and jagged. The respectable Miss ten Boom, with her Victorian manners, must have looked like a poor beggar to the well-groomed officer of the Third Reich who entered her cell.

"Are you strong enough to come to the examination room?" he asked.

Corrie knew, as did all of the prisoners, that a hearing was a thing of terror. The news spread along the cell block: What would happen? Would she betray anyone? Would she be beaten or worse?

The encounter with Hans Rahms, the *Sachbearbeiter,* or judge, was one that left a lasting impression upon Corrie and upon Herr Rahms. He was not a Christian, but a man whose heart was so open to the Gospel that after his first encounter with Corrie, he called her back repeatedly for interrogation.

For the first time in months, there was a touch of kindness from the enemy. The second time Corrie was summoned for a hearing, the handsome judge, with the angular but haunted face, leaned against the wall and said, "I did not sleep all night, but thought constantly of what you told me about Jesus. Tell me more about Him."

Corrie relaxed, in safe territory talking about her Savior, "Jesus Christ is Light, come into the world in order that everyone who believes in Him need not remain in darkness. Is there darkness in your life?"

Betsie was also interrogated in the judge's office, and five times she prayed with him. Hans Rahms became a friend, instead of an enemy, and as a result was instrumental in setting Willem free from Scheveningen and in destroying papers that would have incriminated many underground workers and Jews. He threw all of the evidence into the fire.

At that instant, Corrie understood the verse from Colossians 2:14 (KJV): "Blotting out the handwriting of ordinances that was against us, which was contrary to us, and took it out of the way, nailing it to his cross."

Years later, after the war, Corrie met Hans Rahms in Germany, and he told her: "I have always remembered you and your sister's prayers."

The seeds had been planted, and there was more to come for the judge.

In the summer of 1944 the rumors and whispers of invasion and liberation began to sift through the gray walls at Scheveningen. The world outside was torn by the greatest global war in the history of mankind. The fierce German war machine, which Hitler had been building since he first came to power, was beginning to crumble. The British, American, and French Allies had achieved victory over the Axis in Africa. The Italian army and navy, under the dictator Mussolini, had surrendered. The German submarines were suffering increasing losses in the Atlantic, and the mighty German Luftwaffe was being bombed on the ground and shot down in the air. Everyone knew that planning for the big invasion was underway, under the direction of General Dwight Eisenhower. When would it be?

On June 6, 1944, there was confusion and uncertainty, mixed with vague hope, in the prison in the little seaside Dutch town. Orders to get dressed, take all your belongings, and file into the corridor were shouted. Corrie stumbled out of her solitary cell and, along with the other prisoners, was loaded into a van and driven to a railroad station outside the Hague.

There she saw, among all the prisoners, her dear sister Betsie. They shoved through the mass of frightened women and clung to each other. Nothing seemed too difficult to face when they were together as they had been for more than fifty years.

As the dark train, with its windows shut tight, creaked its way across Holland, a great Allied invasion fleet was on its way from Great Britain to the coast of Normandy, in northern France. It was the beginning of the end of the war—but the beginning of hell for Corrie and Betsie.

11

Factory to Hell

For a brief, euphoric time, Betsie and Corrie believed that their lives would improve. What did it matter that the train was jammed and the air foul? Betsie wrote in her diary, "Corrie and I were together in the train compartment. Everything terribly strict here, but still so grateful not to be in a cell any longer."

The train stopped at 4:00 A.M. Men and women were shoved to the platform and ordered to march through a terror-filled night. Their destination: Vught, a concentration camp in Noord-Brabant, which was built as an overflow camp for Jews as well as a permanent concentration camp for others.

Herded by guns, blinded by floodlights, the weary, weak Hollanders were driven through the forest. When they arrived at the camp, they were shoved into a large hall, only to sit without water or food for twelve hours. *Vught:* The very name was frightening. This place was the scene of a major scandal in 1943, when its commandant ordered seventy-four women locked in a small cell overnight. The next morning, ten women had died of suffocation, and others had gone insane.

On scraps of paper, pieces of toilet paper, whatever she could find, Corrie wrote down sketches of the events of these nightmare times. Did she have any idea that years later they would be published and read in many languages? Was she given some divine insight that the ugly events in their lives would be her undergraduate work for a worldwide classroom?

The women from Scheveningen were put in a separate barracks, outside of the regular camp at Vught. For ten days 150 women were housed in a single room, ordered to sit side by side at tables, doing nothing. Boredom and the accompanying grumbling and criticism crept in. Betsie decided to organize a society. Of course, a group of Hollanders together without a club or society would be unthinkable. The rules were quite simple: "Whoever wishes to become a member must promise to do his utmost not to grumble or complain or speak ill of anyone, but only to speak encouragingly to others. Next, she must resolve to obey all orders of the corridor attendants."

Corrie had a prayer group that prayed daily for the attitude of the women in the society.

When freedom is denied a human being, his personal attitude is balanced by the hope he has. Corrie and Betsie were exhilarated when they were sent a pink form to see the "General" and told, "A pink form always indicates that a prisoner is to be released." They said good-bye to their Society of Hollanders, divided most of their possessions among them, and consoled them that the war could not last much longer, and they would all be free.

The personal items that were confiscated when they entered camp were returned. That was a good sign. They were taken to a building at the main camp exit; their spirits were high. Freedom at last! As they stood in line, the man beside Corrie said, "If any one of you can pray, you'd better do it now."

"We can pray," said Betsie. "Let's do so. But aren't we going to be released?"

"No," said the man. "You'll be brought to the bunkers—or worse."

The bunkers were gloomy cells with small, barred windows. It was there the women had smothered to death and gone insane.

"Evidently the Lord still has work for us to do here," Betsie said and then began to sing:

> I do not fear the dim tomorrow,
> For my Savior holds my hand.
> Strong in Him, I turn from sorrow
> And I face the unknown land.

The "unknown land" was not freedom, but the main camp at Vught. To give prisoners a glimmer of hope and then crush it cruelly was an effective psychological ploy used by the Nazis.

Life was "bearable" in Vught. Corrie organized (of course!) a discussion group "primarily to release our thinking from the narrow confines of camp life." She developed a discussion outline that was entitled "Our Responsibility After This Prison Camp Experience." The discussion questions ranged from, "How can we gain the courage and strength necessary to face the problems," to, "Is it necessary to start thinking now about our lives after camp?" Some of the prison "club members" approached the questions from a theological viewpoint, others from philosophy. Corrie frankly admitted as a discussion it was a fiasco, but at least she had people thinking beyond the boundaries of barbed wire.

Vught was a place of contrasts. Sometimes parcels were allowed to reach the prisoners, and they would have a feast. In the midst of celebration with some goodies from home, there would be a sudden silence as a salvo of shots was heard from the bunkers. A whim, an infraction of the rules, a retaliation, and people were pulled from the cells and executed without warning.

Sometimes, however, when the Brabant skies were ablaze with sunsets, when other prisoners showed friendship, it did not seem that Vught was so bad. However, one precious element was missing: freedom. Corrie said, "One never realizes what that means until he has lived in imprisonment. The bad part of it lay not in the material situation, but in the fact that it was forced upon us by our enemies. There was a constant feeling of helplessness."

One story Corrie told, "It is not so much what happens as how you react to what happens. I studied the behavior of Miep, a girl in Vught. We had to make our beds in a certain way, with the blankets folded so that they made one line over the whole ward. Some people were awkward in doing that, and when it was not correct, the whole room was punished in a cruel way.

"Miep always helped wherever she could. When she saw prisoners struggling with their blankets, she went over the whole room so that the inspection was successful. She was without fear. She could talk to the *Aufseherin* (woman guard) in a way that even influenced her. Just a kind word, a smile, could save the situation. Miep had to suffer just as much as the rest of us, but it seemed that she was not unhappy. Later, in Ravensbruck, when many of us were almost in despair, I will never forget what Miep said: 'We have come through many things. We will also come through living here.' "

As the summer came to an end, hope for release surged again. Rumors were whispered that Hitler had been killed (an unsuccessful attempt to assassinate Hitler had been made on July 20, 1944); the Allies were marching to victory in France and Belgium; the exiled Dutch government, in a London broadcast to the Dutch patriots who were huddled around their forbidden radios, said, "The liberation is at your door, tune in for instructions."

"It's only a matter of days," they were saying. There was excitement, hope, and whispered plans in the camp. Although the guards were nervous and threatened more than ever, no one seemed to be bothered by them. Corrie and Betsie sat at their benches, pretending to work on their assigned tasks of sewing or assembling radio parts, but in reality, talking about nothing but home.

Suddenly, all activity was interrupted by a loudspeaker from the men's camp. Something was happening over there. The women crowded on benches to get a glimpse out of the high windows, through the barbed-wire fence that separated the men's and women's camp.

Over and over they heard names being called. One woman said to Corrie, "Oh, I can see my husband. I'm so afraid they're going to do something awful to him."

The men were called forward and marched out of the gate. Terror seized the women: They waited. Then they heard the sound of guns. They counted one hundred and eighty shots. Corrie wrote: "Every shot meant the death of a good Netherlander. I laid my head on Betsie's shoulder. Could misery become so great that one would collapse under it?"

To Corrie, Betsie looked so serene. What had happened to her? Had God put a hedge about her as He did about Job? Didn't she know what had happened? Corrie prayed, "O Lord, You have borne all our griefs—Will You bear this one?" And the Lord seemed to speak to her heart, "Yes, my child, you cannot bear the sorrows of the world. Cast all your burdens upon Me."

Perhaps that is why Betsie seemed at peace. She had learned that, humanly speaking, the horror of what she was seeing was too much for her to bear. She had given her burdens to her Lord; otherwise, she would go mad! How could anything be worse than the systematic murder of these Dutchmen? Surely nothing the women could experience would equal the mind and soul shock of this scene. How could they know that this was just act one in the ghastly drama which was to follow?

The women's barracks at Vught were scenes of numbing grief. Husbands, sons, brothers, had been executed within earshot of their loved ones. Corrie prayed, "Lord, give me Your Holy Spirit that I may bring this great sorrow to You and leave it with You." Then she remembered a quiet evening in Lunteren, years before, when the Sadhu Sundhar Singh was asked a universal question: "Why did God permit so many innocent people to die in the war?" The Sadhu answered, "Because God thought it necessary."

Corrie realized that God does not make mistakes.

Vught was being emptied before the Allies had a chance to enter Holland. The German rationale was to bring prisoners of war into Germany, where they could provide goods and services that the rapidly depleting German manpower could not supply. The women were herded into boxcars, eighty to a car that had room for forty: no windows, no provision for toilet facilities, very little air. They were packed in so tightly that it was impossible to sit down. Thrown in with the Dutch political prisoners were the girls of the "red-light commando." Their lewd language and swearing made the atmosphere even more horrible.

Tight against Corrie was an *Ehrenbraut*, a girl who had been seized because she infected a German soldier with venereal disease. Corrie told her about the Lord Jesus and then said, "If you ever need my help, will you come to me? I live. . . ." But she didn't know where she would live. The Beje was a memory, perhaps never again to be relived.

At one time, the miserable, parched women thought they heard hailstones on the roof of the car, but then realized that it was machine-gun fire. The train stopped, and Betsie and Corrie gripped each other's hands. They were both calm. Later they found out that it was an attempted rescue, but the effort had been ill planned and thwarted.

The train of cruelty took them deeper into Germany. For three days and three nights they traveled. Corrie felt so ill that she slid into apathy, indifferent to the suffering around her. Betsie, however, looked through holes that had been gouged in the sides of the decrepit cars and reported the devastation of the lovely German towns. Parts of the countryside, however, looked so peaceful that it seemed incongruous that an insane dictator ruled over this lovely land, bringing death and destruction to millions.

When the train finally stopped, the sick, dirty, exhausted women stumbled out, so weakened that it took only a few soldiers to guard them. Corrie noticed that they were just boys, some of them no older than fifteen or sixteen. Was the war going so badly for Germany that children were in the army?

As the Netherlanders marched five abreast through the countryside they saw a contrast that seemed unreal, like a painting in the midst of a slum. There was a lake and, beyond, a little white church, its spire rising against the hills. Corrie thought of the words from the Twenty-third Psalm: ". . . . green pastures . . . beside the still waters." And then the important comfort: "Yea, though I walk through the valley of the shadow of death, I will fear no evil . . . thy rod and thy staff they comfort me" (KJV).

Ravensbruck. It was known as the concentration camp of no return. As the Dutch women marched through the iron gates, one of them started singing:

> We never let our courage lag;
> We hold our heads up high;
> Never shall they get us down,
> Though they be ever so sly.

Even the commander was said to have remarked: "I don't understand these Hollanders. You pack them in boxcars for three days, and they march into camp singing."

Corrie looked at Ravensbruck, the bleakness, the gray and black monotony of color, the emaciated women reaching through bars, with skeletonlike hands, begging for food, and thought, *It does not look as if one could remain alive here.* Many didn't. Thousands died of malnutrition and disease, and thousands more were gassed or otherwise executed.

They were marched first into a huge tent, where Corrie and Betsie found a small space to sit together on the vermin-infested ground. When they saw all the bugs surrounding them, Betsie pleaded with Corrie to cut her hair short. For the first time in many years, the scissors were taken to Betsie's lovely, wavy hair. Corrie buried it in the sand, removing another symbol of dignity.

Ordered out of the tent, made to sleep on the ground, getting soaked during the night by a cold rain, these were just a preface to the book on Ravensbruck that was written for Corrie and Betsie and thousands of others.

For two days and nights they slept outside, waiting for the next order. When it came, it was so starkly evil that Corrie prayed, "O Lord, save us from this evil; Betsie is so frail."

Every possession of the *neue Zugaenge* (new arrivals) was to be taken from them, including their clothing. Then they were to walk, naked, into the showers, and afterwards have prison dress issued.

"Betsie, are you prepared to offer this sacrifice also, if God should ask it?"

"Corrie, I cannot," she whispered.

Corrie didn't know how she could do it herself, but she pleaded with God, "O Lord, if you nevertheless ask this sacrifice of us, give us the willingness to make it."

An officer screamed at them, "Do you have any objections to surrendering your clothes? We'll teach you Hollanders what Ravensbruck is like!"

Their names were called: "ten Boom, Elizabeth; ten Boom, Cornelia." For a few brief moments they prayed, and then Betsie said softly, "Corrie, I'm ready."

They went arm in arm into the terrifying building. First they handed over the few possessions they had. Corrie asked if she could use the toilet, and she and Betsie were pointed to the shower rooms and told to go in the drain holes. Once inside, Corrie said, "Quick, take off your underwear." She and Betsie peeled off their woolen underthings, wrapped the precious little Bible in them, and put the bundle in a cockroach-infested corner.

Corrie was happy. She knew she could not endure life without her Bible, but to the Nazis this was *Das Lügenbuch* (the book of lies). She whispered, "The Lord is busy answering our prayers, Betsie."

As they returned to the row of women waiting to go to the showers, a great sense of peace came over her. They went into the showers, and when they came out were issued shabby clothes and shoes. The fronts and backs of the dresses had crosses cut out and covered with material of another color. If anyone had a chance to escape, the prison garb would be spotted.

Stepping into the showers, many of those women must have felt the harshness of the unknown. Would water or gas come out of the spigots?

Corrie hid the roll of underwear and her Bible under her dress. She bulged in the wrong places as the thin material revealed her hidden treasures. Each woman passed by the guards, inspected from neck to thigh by rough, rude hands. But Corrie prayed, "Lord, cause Your angels to surround me; the guards must not see me."

She felt perfectly at ease as she passed by inspection; it almost seemed as if she were invisible. Even Betsie, immediately following her, was searched. Outside, in the chilling cold of the German autumn, Corrie thanked the Lord for her answered prayer and thought, "O Lord, if you answer my prayers with your angels, I can face even Ravensbruck unafraid."

The Hollanders were quartered first in Barracks 8, the quarantine barracks. It was there that they began to have some comprehension of the hell they faced. Beds were stacked in tiers of three, with anywhere from five to seven women assigned to a bed that was only twenty-seven inches wide. How could they sleep? Lengthwise was impossible, because the ones on the outside would fall off. Corrie said, "We tried lying crosswise. We slept so close together that when one wanted to turn around, all five had to do so."

As I wrote I tried to grasp the depths of cruelty in the concentration camps. I did not want to saturate a biographical account with stories of Nazi atrocities. However, I realized that only through understanding what Corrie and others like her endured, could the remaining years of her life become more significant.

Corrie was once asked, "Why don't you tell more of what really went on in Ravensbruck?" She replied, "It is not important. What is important is that people hear the Gospel."

She never wrote or told the story of how bad it was in that concentration camp. One of her closest friends, the movie director Jimmy Collier, said that he thought God put a protective hedge around Corrie and Betsie, so that the worst memories of her prison-camp experiences would be erased.

While going through some of her old papers and memorabilia, I came across a diary, written in German by a woman who had been in Ravensbruck at the same time. What a gruesome treasure this proved to be!

This Ravensbruck diary described circumstances that even Corrie did not choose to reveal. That poor, unknown woman told about the quarantine block where:

> Our entire possessions consisted of a tin plate, a tin pot, and a wooden spoon—virtually nothing else, not even a

hairpin, washcloth, sewing kit, or anything else. . . . in very short time I was covered from head to toe with large, festering wounds caused by filth, dog bites, and vitamin deficiency. My feet were rubbed raw by the wooden shoes. It was impossible to keep myself clean.

We received one-quarter of a liter of ersatz coffee, which was undrinkable because of the addition of sodium carbonate, and a daily ration of bread (one slice). We were always terribly hungry, while the SS guards were well supplied with everything. They had well-stocked pig, cow, geese, hen, and horse stalls, as well as greenhouses and vegetable gardens. They lacked in nothing; even cigarettes and alcohol were lavishly available. Our SS female guards ate their sausage sandwiches in front of our eyes, drank beer and coffee, while it was impossible to get a cup of tea for even the sickest prisoners.

In the sleeping quarters we lay without sheets or blankets; there were scarcely any windowpanes, thus we were in a constant draft with a view on one side toward a high wall with an electrified wire fence, on the other side, another barracks. The worst thing was the cold; for every morning, often long before daybreak, we stood without coats or any protective covering in the cold. The physical pain brought tears to my eyes. Everything was so arranged as to destroy sensitive persons and those with incurable diseases.

In the first few weeks, Corrie was astonished how Betsie would find a small corner in the barracks and sit serenely, busy mending with precious gifts of needle and thread: She was a woman with the rare ability to create a pleasant atmosphere no matter where she was. Twice a day, Corrie opened her little Bible and invited those who wished to listen. How precious each passage was to them. Corrie said, "What joy it was to share the happy message of God's Word. Paul wrote when in prison with his hands chained to the hand of a guard, "I count everything as loss, compared to the possession of the priceless privilege—the overwhelming preciousness, the surpassing worth and supreme advantage—of knowing Christ Jesus my Lord, and of progressively becoming more deeply and intimately acquainted with Him . . ." (Philippians 3:8 AMPLIFIED).

As suffering built upon torment for the prisoners in Ravensbruck, Betsie seemed to develop around her a shell that blocked out the increasing cruelty. Corrie, in her books and memoirs, describes Betsie as a woman who saw good in almost every circumstance. She thanked God for fleas, which infested the barracks, because they kept the guards from entering; she prayed for the cruel guards as frequently as she did for the oppressed; she was undisturbed by the evil surrounding her. Betsie, although older than Corrie, became like a child, needing Corrie beside her constantly. She would say, "Corrie, don't leave me alone so long."

One of the mindless cruelties of the camp was the daily roll call. The diary account of our unknown Ravensbruck inmate describes this:

> Every morning the siren wailed. I never found out at what time this happened . . . many were of the opinion that it was 2:30 in the morning. At 3:30 we had to fall in for roll call. We stood and stood without being permitted to move until the supervisor had been given the barracks count. I will never forget the first months in Ravensbruck. Every day we heard a small train at morning roll call. In the background stood huge pine and birch trees; the forest appeared in silhouette, and you stood there knowing that the Gestapo had framed you and that if the Third Reich didn't collapse, you would stand there for the rest of your life. You always had dysentery from standing in the cold.
>
> Every day sick, underfed creatures would collapse, whereupon they would be beaten. If they could not get up, they were sent to the office after roll call in order to be "sent to the infirmary," which meant being gassed. You needed permission to leave to go to the bathroom . . . if you could not, you had to run around in soiled underwear, which couldn't be washed. If you were sly enough to wash your underwear and hang it on a clothesline, it would disappear immediately, having been found by the camp police or stolen. Then you would have to try to trade your bread for a new set of underwear.

Sometimes Corrie would take her Bible to roll call, put it against the back of the prisoner in front of her, and quietly read a Psalm or something from one of Paul's letters. Many Psalms were born in misery, and they would take on meaning for the prisoners who were standing close and could hear what she read.

One morning, worn out from standing during roll call, Corrie and Betsie had returned to the barracks and collapsed on the small bed, where five women were pressed tightly together, when the shout came again, "All out for roll call." They stumbled outside, and Corrie reeled from a cruel club blow on her neck. *"Schneller, schneller* [faster, faster]," screamed the guard.

All day they were forced to stand, denied food and water. A weakened prisoner said, "Someone must get through to the *Lagerführer* [camp leader] to report how we are being treated."

"No," uttered Betsie, "that would do no good. We must appeal higher up and ask the *Weltführer* [world leader—God]. Only the Lord can help us."

These ordeals had been deliberately planned by the Lagerführer to break the spirits of the prisoners and weaken their morale. Another degrading trick was the nude parade. The women were forced to stand with hands at their sides, shivering and miserable, while they were examined by the doctors. Corrie recalled the painting of Jesus on Golgotha; although sensitive artists have depicted Him in a loincloth, He was, in fact, completely naked. Corrie thought of how He must have suffered. If God's Son, whose home was heaven, suffered so that someday she, Corrie, might go to heaven, she prayed, "O Savior, You suffered for me on Calvary. I thank You for it. Help me bear this and give me strength."

When they were transferred to Barracks 28, the prisoners again felt hope which was only to be dashed by dismal reality. This new home had 1,400 women crammed into a filthy, cold building meant to house 700. From there, they were forced to march out each day to the Siemens factory, where first they sorted screws; then they were sent outside to push lorries to the railroad station, to unload iron plates from the boxcars, and to push them back to the factory. It was impossibly heavy work for women like Betsie and Corrie. After the morning's work, they returned to the barracks for lunch, and Corrie leaned against a table and went to sleep standing up. As she slept, she dreamed of being home in the dining room. Nollie was there. Together they walked through the house; Corrie saw the antique cupboard, the shop, the display of watches in the window. She sat in Father's chair before the fireplace. Then she awoke in the lunchroom barracks of Siemens. Betsie was beside her, and Corrie laid her head upon her sister's shoulder and sobbed. It was so wonderful to be home, but it was just a dream. She said, "It was one of the rare moments in which homesickness had gotten the better of me."

Even in such depths, there were others who were worse. One day, during a few minutes of leisure, Corrie was walking past one of the barracks and looked through a window into a small, concrete-walled room. She saw a feebleminded child, with no clothing except a short vest. She was almost a skeleton and leaned against the stone wall, with a vacant look in her eyes. Someone told Corrie, "That child has been living here for weeks on half rations; she sleeps at night on the concrete floor, without a mattress or blanket, and yet she can still stand up. How can human life be so tenacious?"

Corrie prayed that she would be released soon; then she would establish a home for feebleminded people, where they would have love and care. "Lord," she prayed, "take this poor child to Yourself quickly, and save the world from this terrible regime."

Corrie did not understand the "why" of suffering, except her own. She knew God had brought her to Ravensbruck for a specific task: to lead the sorrowing and the despairing to the Savior, to point the way to heaven for those who might die at any moment.

Corrie was learning not to rely on her own strength, but to bring her grief to Jesus and leave it with Him. She was also learning to pray as she had never prayed before. But the lessons of love for the enemy were hard. The guards did not seem human; they were animals somehow disguised in the flesh and bones of real men and women.

Everyone knew where the punishment bunkers were; the steady screams and moans could be heard inside. The Ravensbruck diary describes:

> The worst things were the beatings prescribed by the Gestapo. An SS doctor would take the prisoner's pulse. The prisoner was then beaten on the bare body with a rubber club or leather strap until the pulse stopped. I saw the bodies of many of my female companions. They usually collapsed and were then mistreated again after two or three days, until the prescribed number of strokes had been fulfilled.

The work to be done was endless and hard. Corrie was pulled out of the ranks at roll call one morning and marched out the gate, into the woods. On either side of the exit were officers and a number of *Aufseherinnen*. The men looked like wild animals feeding on their prey. When one woman failed to keep her arms stretched out in front of her, an officer pounded on her, dragged her out of line, and beat her cruelly. The other officers looked on with pleasure.

"I shall preserve thy going out and thy coming in," the Bible said. Corrie recalled that promise and found an inner healing. She walked, however, with difficulty. Her feet and legs were swollen with hunger edema, which was a serious abdominal disorder caused by malnutrition. Soon she was ordered to push railroad cars full of potatoes, stumbling under the physical strain.

A guard saw her and sneered, "Oh, perhaps the hands of Madam Baroness are too delicate for such work?"

Corrie looked at herself: coat soiled and frayed, hands covered with parts of worn-out stockings, toes protruding from her broken shoes. She was poorer than the poorest beggar she had ever seen in the Netherlands. She was pushed, pelted with potatoes, and treated with shrieking laughter. Hate welled up within her. Corrie began to look at the guards with anger growing in her heart. Some of them were so young, the ages of her club girls back home. How could they ever be rehabilitated into decent human beings?

Betsie, however, never seemed to allow hatred or bitterness to penetrate her attitude. Her wistful sense of humor prevailed in humorless situations. She gave Corrie God's strength during times when He seemed so remote.

In happier days Corrie used to amuse her family with stories of the wisdom from the mouths of her feebleminded girls whom she loved and taught. One time she was explaining to them the difference between *creating* and *making* by trying to explain how we make things out of wood or stone, but God created the world out of nothing. The Dutch word for "creating" is *scheppen;* the same word, in Dutch, also means "shoveling." When Corrie asked the question of her class, "Does anyone remember what creating [*scheppen*] is?" one of the girls, confusing the unrelated meanings, said, "That is simple, Tante Kees, when we shovel, we need a shovel; God can shovel without a shovel." The answer contained inadvertent wisdom.

When Corrie and Betsie were assigned to a work detail, shoveling sand, the work brought them near their physical breaking point. Betsie found it almost impossible to lift the shovel, let alone fill it with sand. Three of the Gestapo slave drivers surrounded her, viciously insulting her. Their whips were poised to strike her frail body. Suddenly Betsie turned around to Corrie, who was working behind her, and said with a twinkle in her eye, "God can shovel without a shovel."

To Corrie, that unintentional pun of a feebleminded girl became the refrain for her prayer life in the center of this engulfing evil. "Lord, You are all-powerful. I don't know what to do, but I do know that You know all things. You can create well-being, though all the physical conditions for it are lacking."

One time Betsie was vulnerable to the misery surrounding her; the conditions were designed to break the strongest spirits. At 3:30 A.M. they were driven from their beds, to stand for roll call in the *Lagerstrasse*. Ravensbruck at that time contained 35,000 people, a sickening sea of wraithlike humanity. Finally, numb with cold in the German winter, the *Uhle* (siren) sounded to fall out. But the barracks door was locked, and for another forty-five minutes they were kept in the cold, with the Aufseherin guarding the door with a whip. A woman tried to crawl through a window and was beaten unmercifully, while the others watched, petrified with misery.

A feebleminded girl in front of Betsie and Corrie dirtied her pants and was brutally beaten and driven to the ground, a bleeding pulp. An old woman collapsed and died. Corrie looked at the faces around her and read the horror and hate, but also numb resignation and despair.

Betsie leaned against her beloved sister and whispered, "Oh, Corrie, this is hell."

Courage is born in adversity, but Corrie said she was not brave, that she often pulled her dirty blanket over herself and prayed, "Lord I am weak and cowardly and of little faith; hold me close. Thou art the conqueror. Give me courage." From that dependence, that surrender to her Lord, Corrie accomplished feats that were astounding for a woman in her fifties, weakened by malnutrition and ill-treatment.

One night she heard that 250 younger, stronger Dutch prisoners were being transported to a distant factory; destination unknown, return uncertain. In the middle of the night, Corrie went to the washroom, climbed out the window, and stationed herself in the pitch dark in a place where she was sure the prisoners would pass. She prayed, "Lord, give me some word for them." As each one passed, she stage-whispered:

"Jesus is Victor."

"Oh, Corrie, how could you? Go back to your barracks."

"Fear not, only believe."

"Thank you, Corrie. God bless you."

"Underneath us are the everlasting arms."

Corrie told Betsie later, "The Holy Spirit gave me a short message for everyone who went through the gate."

She risked being cruelly punished or killed, but was rewarded after the war when she found out that of the 250, only one did not come back to Holland. A survivor told her later: "Shortly after we arrived, a terrible bombardment shook the area. I was sitting in a corner of a room and couldn't think of anything except what you said: 'Jesus is Victor.' We were unprotected, but our building was not bombed."

Courage does not depend on circumstances, but on the relationship that remains during the circumstances.

Corrie and Betsie had their Bible studies; women found peace and a personal relationship with Christ. As conditions worsened, Corrie's relationship with the Lord she had known all her life became closer and stronger, but it was Betsie who planned for the future. Corrie seemed too absorbed in the here and now to have the vision for life after the death of Ravensbruck.

"Corrie, these barracks are now used to destroy lives. After the war there won't be any use for concentration camps. We must ask God to give us one in that coming time when so many morally wounded people will need care or help. We will use it to build up lives."

Betsie saw things "as it were from His point of view." He gave her spiritual insight and understanding.

Betsie weakened and became seriously ill. Her legs were paralyzed, and Corrie and her friend Mien had to carry Betsie to roll call and support her during the interminable standing. Finally, she was taken to the hospital.

Betsie was not afraid, "Remember, Corrie, we're both going back to Holland; we'll be free before the New Year."

Betsie had a dream (or was it a vision?) about their work in Holland after the war. It was for a house where Dutch people who had been in concentration camps could come to rebuild their lives. The home would be large and beautiful, with polished wood and a garden full of flowers. After they had established it, they would travel over the world, telling people what God had taught them in

Ravensbruck. "We know from experience, Corrie, that the light of Jesus is stronger than the deepest darkness. Wherever there is need, we must help and go wherever He sends us. I can't understand how God will finance it, but He will."

But Betsie's plans, her dreams for the rehabilitation home in Holland, for the worldwide travel, for the reconstructed concentration camp in Germany, seemed to be dying, just as she was.

She was carried on a stretcher to the infirmary, full of hope for the future. Betsie's final words to Corrie were, "Remember now, both of us."

Betsie lived for only two days. When Corrie finally managed to find her body, dumped in the washroom with other skeletal corpses, she saw one of God's miracles in the midst of unspeakable filth. Betsie's face in death looked incredibly young, full of peace, and happy as a child's. It was a bit of heaven in the midst of surrounding hell.

Another woman, our unknown writer of the Ravensbruck diary, was in the infirmary during that same period. Her description adds credence to the conditions of the so-called hospital.

> I got typhus and had to go to the infirmary, which at least was some relief, since I didn't have to report to roll call. It allowed my wounds to heal somewhat better as well. Two times a week we received paper bandages that didn't last five minutes. One often lay together with contagious diseases or deep, open wounds and absolutely no bandages, four or five people on two straw sacks. You even got over being nauseous, you became stoic.
>
> It was especially sad with the blind—they were not permitted to leave their beds, received no care, and almost all died. At first we saw a lot of cripples with crutches and canes . . . later they were all destroyed in the usual way, by gassing.

How could anything good or beautiful come out of these depths?

But Corrie survived. Four days after Betsie died, her number was called. She didn't know whether it meant the death sentence, transport to another camp, or freedom. She said, "I was not afraid to die. The valley of the shadow of death had no terror for me. Jesus had carried me through these prisons. He would stay with me until the end, or better, the new beginning."

It was the end of 1944. In the outside world the war raged. The southern part of Holland was in Allied hands, including the area around Vught, where Corrie was in her first concentration camp. Prince Bernhard, husband of the Crown Princess Juliana, took control of the freed south, but the north remained occupied. Holland was sliced in two.

We do not know why Corrie was chosen for release, except that rumors had been running through that camp that all Hollanders who had been brought to the camp as political prisoners after the entrance of America into the war had been made honorary citizens of the United States. Perhaps the twisted minds of the Nazis thought that they would fare better, in case of defeat, if they began to release prisoners.

After a brief stay in the dreaded infirmary, to try to ease the swelling from her edema-ridden legs, Corrie was released on New Year's Day, 1945. She was given a package containing some of her clothes, brought from Scheveningen, all of which hung on her like a comic scarecrow.

Betsie was right; they were both free by the New Year. But her vision that they would go back to Holland together must have been an illusion of a sick, confused woman. Or was it the vision of someone who heard the direct and divine guidance of God?

As the heavy iron doors to Ravensbruck swung open and Corrie stumbled out, the last words of Betsie rang in her ears. "Remember, now, both of us."

12

From the Smell of Death to a Taste of Freedom

As Corrie pushed one swollen leg ahead of the other on the snow-covered ground between Ravensbruck and the train station in Fürstenberg, the vision of Betsie and her prophetic words rang in her ears. "A home, Corrie, for the broken ones . . . and our message about God's love in this darkness."

How could God use her, a weak, undernourished Dutch woman? As she shuffled along the country road, she passed a labor camp of prisoners. If they lived through the day, they would have to return to the dreaded Ravensbruck barracks that night. Corrie looked at them and felt guilty about her freedom.

She had her gold ring and watch returned and a small sum of money; at least, she thought, she wouldn't go hungry. However, she hadn't realized the importance of food coupons; released prisoners were not issued any, and food could not be purchased without them.

For three days she traveled by boxcar through Germany; the train seemed to creep across the countryside. Once she had to wait hours before transferring to another train. At one stop she saw a piece of white bread on a restaurant table. Starving as she was, she started to take it when a waitress saw her, asked for food coupons, and then ordered her out.

As Corrie continued on her journey, she talked with God: "Lord, I have received my life back from You. Thank You. Will You tell me how to use it? Give me understanding. Yes, Lord, You are right. My work must be to save souls for eternity, to tell about You."

Corrie looked through the window and saw Bremen. Heaps of rubble lay where once there had been comfortable, clean homes. Where was security in this ruined world? She thought of a vision George Fox, the founder of the Quakers, had described: "I saw an ocean of darkness and sin. . . ." Corrie looked at the ruined cities, the concentration camps, the battlefields of war. ". . . But then I saw an ocean of light and love covering that ocean of sin. That was the moment Jesus died on the Cross."

Hungry for food, longing for human love and kindness, Corrie rode her freedom train back to Holland with a promise to her Lord that she would take the message of His love wherever He wanted her to go. Betsie's visions would go with her.

At last she reached Groningen, in the midst of the starvation winter of 1944. The south of Holland was free, under the Dutch military command of Prince Bernhard, but the north and the urban west were in desperate circumstances. There were no Dutch trains running, and the Germans were not about to use their trains to transport food for the Dutch from the rural regions to the city areas.

In Groningen Corrie went to a Christian hospital called the Deaconess Home. For the first time in months she received kindness from people in charge, instead of hatred. Her first food was tea and dry rusk: It tasted like manna from heaven. As she looked at the neat beds in the ward, the clean sheets, the spotless floor, it seemed like a dream. She noticed, however, that the nurses and patients were staring at her and realized that she was an ugly contrast, with her dirty, unkempt, smelly clothes and body. Kindness was such an alien quality that Corrie submitted meekly to every direction.

Her first surprise was in the person of a young nurse who took her to the dining room for her first meal. "Where is your home?" she asked.

"Haarlem," Corrie replied.

"Do you know Corrie ten Boom?"

The nurse was Truus Benes, one of Corrie's YWCA leaders. She didn't recognize this thin, hollow-eyed, dirty woman as the robust, cheerful leader of the Christian Girl Guide movement in Holland.

"I am Corrie ten Boom."

From then on Corrie was treated lovingly, tenderly, by people who cared. The food was plain: brussels sprouts, potatoes, gravy, pudding, an apple, but it was a banquet. She was given a bath, clean clothes, and a bedroom with color. On the shelf were books, and she was provided with a radio. A record of Günther Ramin, playing in a Bach trio, was being broadcast. The memory of that day was so keen that when Corrie wrote her book *A Prisoner and Yet,* she recalled every detail.

After she had been there for ten days, some men from Haarlem came to get some food from the farmers in Groningen. These kind men were generous with their produce and loaded the truck with potatoes, corn, wheat, and meat, to be sent to the West Netherlands, where people were eating sugar beets and tulip bulbs. When it was dark, Corrie left the Deaconness Home, wedged in the cab between two drivers, on a wild ride through Holland. They drove without lights, through the pitch dark, hiding from Allied airplanes and the German Gestapo alike. Their friends bombed every truck, and their enemies confiscated all food. At times the airplanes were so close that they ran from the truck and hid in the shadows along the dikes.

Corrie arrived, shaken but safe, at her brother Willem's in Hilversum. From there she was taken back to Haarlem and the Beje.

Many things had been stolen: some Oriental rugs, her typewriter, the watches and clocks that had been left for repair; but Father's portrait remained, presiding over the dark rooms like an Old Testament prophet. Corrie leaned against Father's bed, thinking about the happiness that he and Betsie were enjoying in heaven. In a deeper sense, they were more at home than she was.

Corrie was changed. She loved all the things she had missed, like her books, music, creature comforts, but she knew that every human worldly security was no security at all. The only security is in the Bible and in the love of Jesus. In Ravensbruck, Corrie could not give in to drowsiness or indifference, because she knew there were people who needed the Lord, people who might die soon. Her constant prayer was, "Speak to me, Lord, give me a message."

Betsie would say to her, "Corrie, you never have spoken more clearly and better than here." Now she was free, and by giving herself she had saved her mind. Her body was weak, and she couldn't walk straight, but her thinking was sharp, and she wanted to share the experiences and the truths the Lord had taught her.

The doors were opened for Corrie's story, but it was a very

cautious opening. It was forbidden by the Germans to tell what had happened in prison, so the meetings were secretive. Many churches had prayed for the ten Boom family, so now Corrie offered to tell them how God had answered their prayers.

As she stood before a church or a small group of believers Corrie had a written speech about the care of feebleminded people in front of her. If the door opened and someone she did not know entered, she would start to speak about the psychology of teaching a child with a low IQ.

The legends of Corrie ten Boom have been built by her admirers, who see her as a fearless, indomitable woman, receiving infallible messages from God for her every act. This picture does injustice to the power of God working with the weakness of man. One headstrong reaction to an experience soon after her return to freedom could have resulted in imprisonment again.

One day Corrie opened the door of the Beje, just as she had hundreds of times before the fateful February raid, and a man made a familiar request.

"Miss ten Boom, I have a friend in prison. You know the director of the prison; he is a good Dutchman and on our side. Will you go with me, introduce me to the director, and ask him to set my friend free?"

Corrie agreed to go, and they climbed onto their bicycles without tires and went to the prison. When Corrie saw the director, she knew she had never met him before. Had she been led into another trap, just as she had with the quisling who had asked for money for his wife? She stumbled through her request for the prisoner and almost panicked when he said, "Wait a moment, I'll phone the Gestapo to see if this request can be approved."

She smelled the prison odor she knew so well and heard a delirious man banging on the door of his cell. A terrible fear gripped her, worse than any she had felt in Ravensbruck.

The prison director took them into his office and closed the door. Then he gave her the harshest—and happiest—scolding she ever received.

"Are you an underground worker? What stupid work you do. You put us all in danger. If I should do what you ask I'd have to hide myself and my helpers immediately. I'll give you advice on how to get this young man out, but don't come here again."

When Corrie was safely home, the man who had requested her

to come with him said, "You looked as pale as death. They told me that Corrie ten Boom was never afraid."

Corrie knew that she was the same woman who climbed out the window in the concentration camp and spoke to her friends who were leaving, the same woman who risked her life with her Bible studies, but she also knew that God had called her to minister in the concentration camp. He was her strength. But this trip was her own desire for adventure, and she plunged ahead without seeking His direction.

From then on her friends forbade her to do any underground work. What about the prison director? Corrie recorded that on the last day of the war he liberated eighteen prisoners who were supposed to be shot and then escaped himself, just in time.

How did Corrie know the leading of the Lord? When she was old, Corrie wrote some books of daily devotions. In one she answered the question about God's will by saying:

> Another way in which God makes us know His will is by closing the doors if our decision is not the right one, or by allowing us to make a mistake, in order that we may see for ourselves that we took the wrong turn when we did not listen to Him. His word tells us that we can hear His voice: "And your ears shall hear a word behind you, saying, 'This is the way, walk in it . . .'" (Isaiah 30:21 RSV).

God clearly led Corrie to speak about her experiences in Ravensbruck and to tell of God's power and strength in times of life's severest hardships. The requests began to come from friends in Haarlem. When she spoke, she told about Betsie's visions. First, for a home, a beautiful place with polished wood banisters, a flower garden, a home for people who had suffered during the war. The most important part of Corrie's task, however, was to tell everyone who would listen that Jesus is the only answer to the problems that are disturbing the hearts of men and nations.

A letter from a prominent Hollander gives us a glimpse into the beginning of that journey through the decades, which was to take Corrie to sixty-four different countries and to speak before millions of people. Jan van der Hoeven, who described himself as "barrister at the Court of Haarlem," a member of the aristocracy, told how Corrie came to their house in March of 1945 for a small gathering of people to tell of her experiences. He wrote:

There was Corrie, who only a short time ago returned from this unbelievable horror—from a hell from which no return seemed possible—speaking about these experiences and at the same time about the love and nearness of the Lord. She was already speaking about a dream her sister Betsie and she had for a home where victims of this terror could be rehabilitated.

When she spoke in the home of that important personage, a five-year-old boy sat and listened. He was Jan Willem van der Hoeven, a little war baby who remembers listening to Tante Corrie in a room with closed curtains, so the Germans wouldn't know there was a meeting inside.

Jan Willem remembered that occasion, and when he was thirteen years old began to read Corrie's letters, which she wrote in a Dutch Christian magazine called *Kracht van Omhoog* (Power From on High). Even as a child, he began to pray for Tante Corrie. This young man was later to have a worldwide ministry himself and become the keeper of the Garden Tomb in Jerusalem, where thousands of Christian travelers visit each year.

As a pebble is dropped in a pool of water and the ripples spread to endless concentric circles, Corrie's worldwide ministry began to take place. The little Dutch boy who first lingered at that adult meeting in Haarlem loved Tante Corrie, as all children did, and emulated the love and concern for the Jewish people that the ten Booms showed. Jan Willem opened the International Christian Embassy in Jerusalem in 1980, which had as one of its primary goals to show concern for the Jewish people and the State of Israel, according to the biblical command in Isaiah 40:1 (RSV): "Comfort, comfort my people, says your God."

After the war there was a housing shortage in every European country, but this was only one of the challenges Corrie faced in her quest to see the fulfillment of the first part of Betsie's vision. With the help of some friends, she found a home, *Schapenduinen,* in the middle of parklike grounds in Bloemendaal, that could be rented for her refugee work. It was the home of the vision: beautiful polished wood, a garden, and quiet rooms for those broken and disturbed lives that God would lead to its doors.

As Corrie plunged into this new project, forming committees to persuade people to give furniture and clothing, she began to receive many invitations from all over Holland to give lectures and tell her experiences of the reality of Jesus Christ in a concentration camp. She always told about Betsie's vision of the home for displaced people and ex-prisoners from the camps. The collection plate was passed, and she urged people to give generously.

In later years Corrie was convicted that she should never ask for money, but during this period she said, "The Lord had not yet told me this."

Mies Poley, the wife of Hans, who had been the first *onderduiker* at the Beje during the war, visited Corrie in the Beje during this time and said that she seemed so lost there. She had taken in a retarded child, who followed Corrie like a shadow. But the house with the crooked stairs seemed hollow. Schapenduinen received most of her furniture. Soon she sold her watchmaker's business, rented the Beje, and used the rehabilitation house as home base.

Corrie had some able assistants in her work. She seemed to be able to attract and inspire people with many talents: Henk van de Bunt had helped find the house; Aad Geels, an able home and camp director, led the work of general administration; a psychiatrist off-ered his time and help without charge. A man who owned a rare item in Holland at that time—an automobile—came to Corrie with an unusual request. He said, "Will you please take my car? May I be your chauffeur? I will pay for the gasoline. All I will need is for my wife and me to use it occasionally."

So her ministry began to grow. First Schapenduinen, where her personal direction exasperated the volunteer psychiatrist. He asked her one day about a deeply disturbed ex-prisoner, and Corrie replied, "Oh, he's getting on fine. Last night he saw the moon shining and climbed out of the window and took a long walk through the dunes. He didn't get back until five in the morning! I said to him, 'Wasn't it a joy, Jan, to be out of prison and go wherever you like, even during the night?' "

"But, Miss ten Boom, how could you? Your patients must be helped to lead a regular, disciplined life. How can you direct such a house when you allow such irregularities?"

The psychiatrist had never been in prison! Corrie had. When she ran the phases of the underground work, she was disciplined and forceful, but after Ravensbruck, she could not exert disciplinary methods upon the ex-prisoners.

On May 5, 1945 all of the Netherlands was free. Dutch flags flew again, the national anthem was heard, and people wept. In the evening, lights were seen from the houses, and people walked in the streets. The royal family returned from exile, and "Long live Wilhelmina," echoed through the country.

Queen Wilhelmina, who was influential in strengthening her subjects, wrote: "I knew myself to be at one with all at home in the invisible and occasionally unrecognizable Guidance whose hand controls the destiny of nations, out of the reach of even the most unscrupulous conqueror."[23]

But in any war there are those who never return. More than 140,000 Dutch died in the resistance, in German reprisal killings, concentration camps, air raids, or from hunger.[24]

Victory was no sooner proclaimed than the treatment of traitors was considered. Some were tried before special courts and sentenced to prison. Some were shot for high treason. Much of the conversation among the Dutch populace concerned the attitude toward their fellow citizens who had betrayed them.

A few weeks after the victory celebration, Corrie was told the name of the man who turned her family over to the Gestapo. How should she react? The copy of a letter she wrote on June 19, 1945, conveys the attitude she had, which God used to share His love and forgiveness around the world.

She wrote:

> Dear Sir:
>
> Today I heard that most probably you were the one who betrayed me. I went through ten months of concentration camp. My father died after ten days, my sister after ten months of imprisonment.
>
> What you meant to be harmful, God used for my good. I have become closer to Him. A severe punishment is awaiting you. I have prayed for you that the Lord will accept you if you will turn to Him. Think about the fact that the Lord Jesus also carried your sins on the cross. If you accept that and will be His child, you will be saved forever.
>
> I have forgiven you everything; God will forgive you everything also, if you ask Him. He loves you, and He, Himself, has sent His son to earth to forgive you your sins, that is, to bear the punishment for you and me. From your side an answer must be given. When He says: "Come to me, give your heart," then your answer must be: "Yes, Lord, I will. Make me your child."
>
> If you have difficulty praying, ask then if God will give

you His Spirit; He works the faith in your heart. Never doubt the love of the Lord Jesus. He stands with His arms wide open to receive you.

I hope that the hard road that you now have to go will bring you to your eternal Savior.

Before she wrote that letter, Corrie confessed she felt an initial surge of hatred and bitterness come into her heart. Then she remembered the words of Jesus: "For if you forgive men when they sin against you, your heavenly Father will also forgive you. But if you do not forgive men their sins, your Father will not forgive your sins" (Matthew 6:14, 15 NIV).

God had established the music for Corrie's symphony. She began to put together the components of her orchestra as one person after another was led to join. For fourteen years Schapenduinen served as the location for mending lives and teaching the Word of God.

Reverend Spencer De Jong, minister at Melodyland Christian Center, in California, recalled how the Youth for Christ team arrived in Holland in 1946, reaching out to minister in a country devastated by massive bombings and the aftereffects of Nazi occupation. Soon after their arrival, the name of Corrie ten Boom was mentioned as one who would help them. The team was short of personal workers to help with new converts. The Reverend De Jong said that in Rotterdam alone almost one thousand people came forward to commit their lives to Jesus Christ.

Corrie's big home in Schapenduinen became a weekend-conference center to train the Youth for Christ workers. Corrie would tell her story, so fresh with its poignancy, and the young people would sit on the floor in the large living room of the house and listen.

De Jong preached in twenty-nine cities in the Netherlands and said: "Even though Corrie could not always be present, we could depend on her for moral and prayer support. She has always been an inspiration to me. She didn't seek for greatness. Her humility was her greatness. The crowds that came to hear her speak sensed her humility, as well as appreciating her humor. Her messages were always forthright, because Jesus was speaking through her."

In 1947, a young Dutch woman, Lotte Reimeringer, came to work for Corrie. She remembers the Bible-study weekends where young people who had accepted Jesus in one of the Youth for Christ rallies came to the large house to learn from this lovable Dutch lady.

Corrie's experience with Girl Guides and clubs, before the war, was valuable.

The needs in Europe were so great. The American war effort had swung the tide of the war, and now Europe looked to America to help design the structure for a new beginning.

After the work began to run smoothly in Bloemendaal, Corrie knew that she was almost ready to obey the second part of Betsie's vision and God's command to tell the world about His love and forgiveness. Where should she go first? God clearly told her: America.

People have said, "That's nonsense. There's no such thing as direct guidance from God. You have to use common sense." When Corrie confronted this type of skepticism, she would remember a verse her parents were given when they were married: "I will instruct thee and teach thee in the way which thou shalt go: I will guide thee with mine eye" (Psalms 32:8 KJV).

A year after her release from prison, God's merry saint, as Billy Graham called her in later years, left Holland on a freighter, with fifty dollars in her pocket, to be a personal missionary to that vast area of the world called America.

Watch out. Here comes Corrie with a story to tell. An American visiting in Haarlem told her, "It's not easy to make one's way in America."

"I believe you," Corrie answered, "but God has directed me, and I must obey."

Corrie and Nollie, properly dressed for church in their Sunday best, 1906. *Below*: The quiet years of study and work, 1906: Betsie, Corrie, Nollie, and Willem.

Beneath the proper exterior were mischievous hearts: Betsie, Nollie, Corrie, in 1907. *Right*: The ten Boom sisters: Who would guess how poor they were in their elegant dresses?

The family in a serious mood, with Tante Anna supporting the ailing Tante Jans. *Right*: St. Bavo's, where Corrie attended church as a child and once heard Albert Schweitzer play the magnificent organ.

A watchmaker must have steady hands. Jeanette Clift as Corrie, in *The Hiding Place*. (Photo courtesy of World Wide Pictures.) *Below*: Corrie always marched to a different drummer: in her Girl Guide days.

Corrie, the magic storyteller, with her girls. *Below*: Mies and Hans Poley, after Hans became a part of the Beje gang as the first underdiver.

Papa, Betsie, and Corrie, with
their Jewish underdivers at
the beginning of the war.
Right: Willem, Corrie's intellectual brother who warned
of the coming persecution of
the Jews.

Kik, Willem's son, who died in a concentration camp in 1944. *Below*: The movies could not convey the horror of Ravensbruck. Here is Jeanette Clift as Corrie, sharing God's love in the concentration camp. (Photo courtesy of World Wide Pictures.)

Herded onto cattle cars, the women were transported to Germany and the concentration camps. Julie Harris, as Betsie, in *The Hiding Place*. (Photo courtesy of World Wide Pictures.)

After the war, Corrie knew God was calling her to take the story of His love and forgiveness to the world. (Photo by R.M. Fronske, Flagstaff, AZ.)

Corrie and Peter, her nephew, sharing experiences in Switzerland. *Below:* With Hans Rahms, the German judge whom Corrie led to the Lord.

Corrie and Peter after the war. *Below*: In Da Nang, Vietnam, telling her story around the world.

When she spoke behind the Iron Curtain, the audience was small, but her message never changed. *Below*: Corrie's first traveling companion-secretary, Conny.

The premier of *The Hiding Place*, the night the tear-gas bomb stopped the show. (Photo courtesy of World Wide Pictures.) *Below*: Corrie and Billy Graham, whose lives enriched each other. (Photo by Russ Busby.)

Oftimes He weaveth sorrow, and I in foolish pride, forget He sees the upper, and I the underside. *Below*: With some prisoners at San Quentin.

God's merry saint.

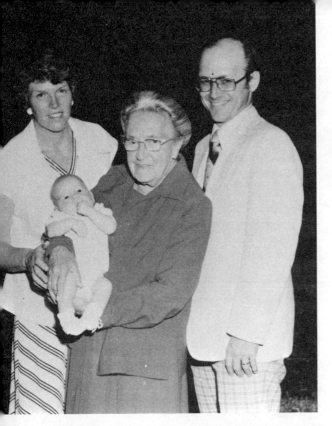

Ellen and Bob Stamps with Peter and Tante Corrie, proud surrogate grandmother. *Below*: "Pam and I make a great team."

As Corrie weakens, Pam Rosewell and Lotte Reimeringer are her constant companions. (Photo by Russ Busby.)

Part III

Visions and Directions

They are called the survivors—those valiant souls who boomerang back from incredible blows may be sources of amazement or discouragement. What do they have that others lack? What substance of grit or stamina has been given to them that is not available to the ordinary person, just plodding through life from one crisis to another?

The Bible says, ". . . these things happened to them as an example, and they were written for our instruction . . . (1 Corinthians 10:11). No novelist could write fiction to compare with Corrie's response to the directions given to her by God. No mere coincidence could account for the ways in which Corrie's and Betsie's visions became realities.

From one of history's darkest hours has come a message for us: "Be strong, and let your heart take courage, All you who hope in the Lord" (Psalms 31:24).

13

Mission: U.S.A.

The first stop on her three-decade world tour began in New York City. Corrie arrived with a slim purse, no place to stay, and her rolling Dutch accent. Hardly an auspicious beginning for a speaking ministry! However, the YWCA had an international language of outreach, and she found a room there for a week.

During the first few days, she spoke to several groups of Jewish immigrants who had come from Germany. When the initial seven days were up, the clerk at the Y asked where Corrie wanted her suitcases sent. She answered confidently, "The Lord has another room for me; I just don't know the address yet."

Corrie knew that the God who led her through Ravensbruck would see her through America.

The puzzled clerk, who encountered many strange people, gave her a skeptical look, reached into the mailbox, and said, "Oh, by the way, here's a letter for you."

No one knew where Corrie was staying, so she was surprised, herself. The letter was from a Jewish woman who had heard her speak, and knowing that it was almost impossible to get a room in New York, she offered Corrie a place in her house as long as she wanted it.

"Oh, yes, here is the address the Lord has for me," Corrie immediately told the astonished clerk, who was not as experienced in "miracles" as this certain Dutch lady.

For five weeks Corrie stayed with the hospitable friend, a time she spent in looking up addresses given to her in Holland and in telling her experiences. She found some people polite, some indifferent, and some pointedly hostile. She was told that too many Europeans were coming to America and that the immigration authorities should put a stop to it. Even some church people questioned her "direct guidance from God."

Her doubts began to grow. She had saved a small amount of money in Holland, but she couldn't bring that to America. Nobody seemed to want to hear her message. Was coming to the United States really God's guidance? She "had a long consultation with my heavenly Father, reciting all my troubles," as she described in her book *Not Good if Detached.*

"Father, if I must borrow money to return to Holland, people will say, 'There, you see, the promises of the Bible are not really meant. Direct guidance does not exist.' Father, for Your own honor's sake, You must help me out!"

The following Sunday, Corrie went to a church where she found the minister was friendly, and he gave her the address of Irving Harris, the editor of *The Evangel,* a monthly Christian magazine. She visited Harris, and again told her story. The editor was impressed and asked, "Would you have anything for me to print in my magazine?"

Corrie gave him the only speech she possessed, and Harris wanted to publish it. However, he added, "I am terribly sorry, but I don't have any money to give you. Everything done for our magazine is without pay."

Corrie answered, "What a joy to meet an American who is not dollar minded!"

Later Harris told Corrie that he thought she would be very disappointed when he said, "No money." Instead, her face was beaming. However, he gave her counsel and introductions, which proved better than money. When she unburdened her doubts and struggles, Harris said, "Pay no attention to those who do not believe in guidance. The Bible contains many promises that God will lead those who obey Him. Have you ever heard of a Good Shepherd who didn't lead His sheep?"

Corrie was given a letter of introduction by Harris to a man in

Washington, D. C., who proved to be a key figure in the start of her American ministry. His name was Abraham Vereide, the founder of the International Christian Leadership, which provided the spring-board for many organizations and outreaches throughout the world, including such traditions as the Presidential Prayer Breakfasts.

Dr. Vereide was a Methodist minister who became concerned about government corruption; in 1942 he moved to Washington to establish a type of Christian embassy called Fellowship House. He was ruggedly handsome, a great man of prayer, and a person who gained access to people in positions of influence, including the highest government officials.

It was this man who invited Corrie to dinner. Here she was, with no funds, poor English, and seated at the table with three university professors. She said, "I felt like a schoolgirl invited out by her headmistress." But Corrie listened and learned. When Vereide spoke about a relationship with Jesus, he showed a train ticket that said, "Not good if detached." Corrie chose those words as a slogan and ten years later wrote a book with that title.

When Vereide introduced this august group of highly educated people, remembering everyone's title, he came to Corrie and said, without hesitation, "This is Corrie ten Boom, a graduate of the University of Ravensbruck."

Through this man, who counseled with presidents, the little Dutch woman with her urgent message for the world began to meet other women who helped her spread her story. First she talked to a small group who met for a weekly Bible study and prayer meeting. One woman gave Corrie a check that enabled her to return money she had borrowed in New York and have some left over. She met people who became lifelong friends and for the next thirty years, opened doors for her in America.

One of those women, Marian Johnson, the niece of President Franklin Delano Roosevelt, was a wealthy, influential Christian who met Corrie at Fellowship House. Mrs. Johnson was ill at the time and said, "Corrie came up to my bedroom, and I could feel the power when she prayed over me." Shortly after that, Mrs. Johnson was the benefactor who gave Corrie the funds she needed to travel in the States and bring her message wherever she was invited to speak.

Alicia Vereide, Abraham's daughter, helped Corrie from the be-ginning and called upon another influential American woman, Mrs.

Frank McSherry, the wife of General McSherry, to act as chauffeur for Corrie, who was receiving speaking requests with increased frequency.

From starvation to Washington society in a few months was a jump Corrie found difficult. She told Mrs. McSherry that she wanted her to schedule three talks a day, so she "wouldn't waste the Lord's time." One speaking engagement Mrs. McSherry arranged was at the National Cathedral School, a prestigious girls' school.

The hall was filled with several hundred girls when Corrie walked down the aisle, a stocky woman with a shapeless black bag. The girls began to whisper, "Oh no—another one of those missionaries!" But not for long! The moment Corrie began to speak, they were all attention. She told of her time in Ravensbruck, about Betsie and her vision of the beautiful home for ex-prisoners, about God's love in the midst of despair—a message she was to repeat hundreds of times. When she was finished, the vaulted ceiling echoed with applause. Mrs. McSherry recalled, "The atmosphere of the hall was electric with spiritual power."

Before the meeting, Corrie asked the Washington society and government wives to pray that her audience would see Jesus, not her, when she spoke. After her address at the National Cathedral School, she received a letter from her hostess: "Your prayer was answered. The girls took a dim view of your charms when they first saw you, but when you began to speak, they knew a greater one than any mortal spoke through you."

When people are asked about Corrie, they tell you stories. Rarely do you have a subjective reaction in general terms, such as, "She's delightful," or, "she's an interesting person." They recall occasions and circumstances that are cemented in their memories for years.

Corrie asked one of the Washington ladies to take her to a public-speaking class, which was popular among the senators, congressmen, diplomats, and other Washington residents who wished to present their experiences and ideas effectively. The teacher of this class had Eleanor Roosevelt, for instance, as one of the pupils. The students were welcome to bring guests, who would be asked to talk about themselves and what their purpose was in being in Washington.

A three-minute limit was established for each speech, after which a critique of each talk was written by the participants and submitted to the teacher, who would make comments to help the speaker improve his or her techniques. The class was varied, and Corrie's hostess was apprehensive about how her guest would be accepted.

Corrie walked to the lectern with her Bible, opened it, and began to read. Her audience was enthralled and sat in absolute silence when she finished. No slips of paper were handed to the teacher, who was a strict Unitarian. The teacher said, "You have an amazing spiritual presence. We all felt it the moment you stood before us." Then she added, "There is only one suggestion I can make. Look at your Bible less and your audience more. You know the words you are reading by heart, so only glance at them and don't lose eye contact with your audience."

Corrie was a learner. She never ceased to ask questions and improve herself.

Her first trip to America began with despair and ended in outreach. In ten months she spoke in churches, prisons, universities, schools, and clubs. She met people who presented her to others and caused her feeble little ministry to multiply. Abraham Vereide introduced her to people who became influential in the years to follow: friends like Katie Cheney, the woman who became a catalyst in later evangelistic campaigns in Bermuda; ministers like Dr. Edwin Orr, the man whose team Corrie joined for a Christian outreach in Australia and New Zealand.

The seeds were beginning to be sown that would grow into an immense harvest, but not without weeds. Finances were always precarious; when Corrie first began to talk, she would tell about the need in Holland and ask people to support her work financially. In general the Americans were very liberal. People did not seem to think it strange when a speaker from Europe asked for collections, but Corrie began to think there was something wrong with it.

One day she was speaking about the financial need for her work among the mentally and physically war-damaged people, and after the meeting a very dignified, well-dressed woman gave her a sizable sum of money.

"It was so interesting to hear about your work," she said.

Corrie answered, "What about the other things of which I spoke? I also spoke on conversion. God does not want only a little of our money; He wants our hearts."

The woman reacted to her gospel message very coolly and left the room without making any comments.

When Corrie returned to her room, she looked sadly at the money she was given. She began to think, *Is there something wrong in speaking of one's own work, and at the same time of the need for conversion?* When she prayed, the answer was clear: "From now on you must never ask for money."

After that, her personal expenses and those of the works she later founded under the auspices of the Ten Boom Foundation were carried out without great pleas for funds. They operated by faith.

The next day Corrie received two letters, one from a woman in Switzerland and one from Nollie in Holland. Both of them said, "When I prayed for your work this morning, God made it very clear to me that you should not ask anybody for financial support. He will provide everything."

Corrie's first ten months in America were truly a great learning experience. Then she began to sense a definite leading for another area. When she left Ravensbruck, she had said, "I'll go anywhere God sends me, but I hope it is never to Germany."

In America, when she no longer seemed to receive guidance, she prayed "Lord, am I disobeying You in some way?"

The answer came clearly. "Go to Germany."

From the comfort and warmth of her new American friends, to a land broken and filled with jagged memories. How could she do it?

"Yes, Lord, to Germany also."

14

Why Germany, God?

The prizefighter, self-assured, well trained, confident of victory, was down for the count. Bloodied and disfigured by combat, his mind was dulled by constant, insistent blows. This was Germany after defeat. The wounds and scars of war were both visible and internal. Into this atmosphere came Corrie, fresh from her recent acceptance in America.

Sorcery and witchcraft abounded in Germany after the war; in days of uncertainty, when the fate of their loved ones was unknown, many wives and mothers visited fortune-tellers. When Corrie returned to the country that had so recently been the home of her enemies, she came with the message of forgiveness, but also with warnings about the power of Satan in the lives of those who were involved in occultic practices.

With the help of German Christians, she was invited to speak at many meetings. Whenever she had a full week of talks in one place, she reserved one evening to prove from the Bible the sin of dealing with such practices as Ouija boards, crystal balls, or palm reading. She took her text from Deuteronomy 18:10–12 (NAS):

There shall not be found among you anyone who makes his son or his daughter pass through the fire, one who uses

divination, one who practices witchcraft, or one who inter-
prets omens, or a sorcerer, or one who casts a spell, or a
medium, or a spiritist, or one who calls up the dead. For
whoever does these things is detestable to the Lord; and
because of these detestable things the Lord your God will
drive them out before you.

Corrie would complete her warning message by saying that we
need not remain in the dark, because Jesus is the Light of the world.

However, a strange reaction took place in Corrie whenever she
gave this message: She became so tired she could scarcely stand up,
and her heart would accelerate wildly. One evening she prayed: "I
cannot continue like this, dear Lord, why must I testify against this
particular sin? So many of Your faithful servants never mention it.
I can't go on like this much longer and live. Perhaps another month
or two, and then my heart will give out."

Corrie's prayers were always direct and precise. Her requests were
specific. Soon after she read in a German book of daily readings,
"Though all the powers of hell attack, fear not, Jesus is Victor."

She realized that the fear of demons comes from demons themselves. "Jesus is Victor" became the theme for her life and the title
for a series of books she wrote many years later.

Casting out demons is a subject that is frequently avoided in
church circles, particularly in America. Corrie became familiar with
this practice in many lands during her subsequent travels. The first
mention, however, that she made of these experiences was during
this postwar period in Germany.

Spencer De Jong recalled that on one occasion in Indonesia, he
was present when Corrie was casting out demons. He said, "In one
case the odor was so vile, every window in the church had to be
opened."

Corrie told of another experience in a small town in Germany
when she was with a group of students for a weekend. Each Christian brought an outsider to the retreat; one of them, a medical
student by the name of Trudy, followed Corrie up to her room after
one of the meetings, to talk further with her. After listening to
Trudy for a while, Corrie suddenly turned to her and commanded
the demons within her to leave in Jesus' name. Immediately the
young student said she felt a great relief and confessed that until
that moment she had contemplated committing suicide.

When Corrie went downstairs to tell her young Christian friends that Trudy was free from the influence of demons, she found out that they had been praying for them from the time they saw Trudy go upstairs. Corrie said, "Keep praying. She is not entirely free."

Is this a special power that God gives to some? How valid is it? Corrie said, "I am well aware I do not possess the special gift to cast out demons, but in times of emergency we must dare to lay hold on the promise of Mark 16:17 [KJV], ". . . in my name shall they cast out devils. . . .' "

Corrie wrote in *Each New Day,* "We need not fear demons, although they often try to bring fear into our hearts. Never forget that those who are with us are stronger than those who are against us. The weapons of our spiritual warfare are the power of the blood of Jesus and the use of His wonderful name."

Emotions were taut in postwar Germany. Corrie met with many who suffered severely from guilt. For instance, in a railway station she gave her suitcase to a boy to carry, and a man came up to her and whispered, "We Germans are all thieves; don't trust that boy." Before she reached her train, five different Germans had warned her. God seemed to be confirming that He wanted her to carry His message of forgiveness into this wounded country.

Before Betsie died, she had said, "Concentration camps are now used to destroy people. After the war there will be no use for them. We must ask God to give us one, and we will use it to build up lives." The memory of her dead sister was kept alive through the visions and directions she had given to Corrie during their prison-camp incarceration.

German friends helped Corrie rent a former concentration camp in Darmstadt, with room for about 160 refugees. Soon it was full, and they had a waiting list.

During those first few years after the war, many Germans seemed drained of energy. They had lost face among the nations of the world; their homes had been destroyed; and they experienced despair when they heard the enormity of Hitler's crimes. Many German citizens were unaware of the mass killings and purges.

Corrie worked with the refugee program of the Lutheran Church on refurbishing Darmstadt. Barbed wire disappeared, flowers appeared in window boxes, and cheerful paint was applied to the drab, gray buildings. Local pastors and church members helped with the building projects. Corrie's work was to finance the camp and visit the people.

She had vowed never again to plead or ask for money, no matter how needy a project she had. However, this didn't mean that she couldn't mention these needs in influential places, did it? In a note-book where Corrie recorded her descriptions of 7,000 slides that she took around the world, she wrote under a picture of Darmstadt: "I went to England and spoke about this camp. I put my needs before the people there."

Those needs must have been met, for Corrie financed and minis-tered in the former concentration camp in Darmstadt for fourteen years. She would travel around the world and return to Holland and Germany about every two years.

Her purpose in Darmstadt was to help people find security in Jesus Christ in the midst of the insecurity of building a new exis-tence among the war ruins. To meet these refugees was to come into intimate contact with bruised Germany: Some were bitter, most were defeated and unhappy. Corrie told about a woman who had been a professor of music in a Dresden conservatory. As they talked together, she found out that Corrie loved Bach. The musician told her that a minister had a piano which he said she could play. It was out of tune, but had been saved after a bombing and left outside in the rain. She asked, "What would you like me to play for you?"

Corrie said, "The 'Chromatic Phantasy' of Bach."

On the damp, broken piano, she played Bach as only a master could do. Corrie ached for this skilled pianist who said, "I had a beautiful home, but it is now destroyed. I had to flee from Dresden and couldn't take one thing with me."

Without the Ravensbruck experience, Corrie would not have been as strong a witness, but she told the professor what she had learned in the hell of prison: that God's love still stands when all else has fallen. She said, "Paul, when he was in prison, lost every-thing, and he wrote to his friends, '. . . I count everything as loss compared to the possession of the priceless privilege—the over-whelming preciousness . . .—of knowing Christ Jesus, my Lord . . .'" (Philippians 3:8).

Hatred and self-pity were other emotions the refugees ex-perienced. She met a lawyer who had lost both legs during the war. He had once been a loyal churchgoer, but now felt that he had been dealt a terrible injustice and was bitter against God and men. Corrie knew what bitterness was. She told the lawyer, "Once I helped a man who said he wanted to liberate his wife. I gave him money. That man was a quisling. He betrayed our family so that we were all sent to prison, where three of us died. When I was in a concentration camp, a prisoner who came from my hometown told me that it was that man who had betrayed me. A strong hatred came into my heart. That is why I can understand you so much."

Corrie told him of Matthew 6:14, 15 (RSV), which says, "For if you forgive men their trespasses, your heavenly Father will also forgive you; but if you do not forgive men their trespasses, neither will your Father forgive your trespasses."

She said, "I did what every Christian can do when he is tempted, for with the temptation we get a way to escape. When we repent, God forgives and cleanses us. Not only was I given forgiveness, but Jesus filled me with the Holy Spirit, and the fruit of the Spirit is love, even for our enemies. When that man was sentenced to death after the war, I corresponded with him, and God used me to show him the way of salvation."

Corrie, without the experience of being betrayed, could not have been used to help erase hatred. A year after this conversation she was in Darmstadt again, and this time the legless man, with his own special car, was at the station to meet her and take her to the camp. Corrie looked apprehensive about going with a legless chauffeur, but he quoted back to her, "You taught me 'Jesus is Victor.' Now you may not be afraid."

This man had surrendered his bitterness, and the Lord had filled his heart with love. He was now working in the refugee camp and said, "God can use even a legless man, when he is surrendered."

Corrie knew that her reluctant acceptance of God's leading her back to Germany was a matter of obeying, not necessarily personal desire. As she experienced the discipline of her obedience, working in Germany became a joy to her. She enjoyed working with the ministers in various churches. Although she experienced doctrinal differences, she said: "Our common aim unites us . . . that of winning souls for eternity, and helping the children of God to learn that 'Jesus is Victor.' "

However, when Corrie was asked to speak at a meeting comprised entirely of ministers, she sometimes encountered her greatest opposition. On one occasion, a large group of German ministers invited her to speak. Her mischievous wisdom erupted in her remarks: "Gentlemen, I am a lay person, a lay woman, a Dutch lay woman. Are there some present who would rather not remain?

"I intend to speak about conversion. Perhaps you have a label for me . . . a Pietist? I shall speak about the Lord's return: that should label me a Sectarian. I may even speak about the Rapture of the Church: that makes me a fanatic; or the fulness of the Holy Spirit: a Pentecostal. Keep your labels handy, gentlemen. Should my words touch your consciences, you have only to label me, set me in a corner, and have nothing to fear."

Anyone who has ever seen Corrie "in action" can imagine how her twinkling blue eyes could persuade the most critical faces to relax.

Corrie encountered one of her biggest challenges in Berlin. Many meetings were planned for her, and at the close of each talk she would counsel with people one at a time. One evening she was tired and very impatient. A man stood in the corner of the inquiry room and waited until everyone had left. When Corrie looked at him, she thought, *I wouldn't like to meet him in a dark street when I was alone.* Finally she turned to him, anxious to end her counseling and go home.

"How can I help you?" she asked.

He looked down and didn't answer. Corrie became sharper in her tone. "Listen, sir, there are many people still waiting. If you won't speak up, I don't know how to help you."

When she saw the despair in his face, she regretted her attitude and started to silently pray for wisdom during the rest of the conversation.

When he spoke, Corrie knew why he was so hesitant. Her body stiffened as he said, "I am one of the guards of Ravensbruck. I was there at the time that you were one of the prisoners. At Christmas time I accepted Jesus Christ as my Savior. I repented of my sins, but then I asked, 'God give me the opportunity to ask one of my victims forgiveness.' That's why I'm here. Will you forgive me?"

Corrie said she felt a surge of hatred in her heart, but then she remembered that the Lord had said, "I forgive you everything." In obedience to Him she reached out her hand to grasp the hand of that guard; it was as if God's love flowed through her. "I forgive you," she said and then opened her Bible. She read 1 John 1:7, 9: "In these verses it is written that your sins are forgiven. Isn't it a joy that we may believe it?"

The former concentration-camp guard covered his face and sobbed, "But I can't forget my sins."

Corrie's simple but biblically sound explanation was "Jesus will blot out your sins like a cloud. A cloud does not return. He will put your sins away as far as the east is from the west. If you repent, He casts them into the depths of the sea, forgiven and forgotten. Then He puts out a sign, NO FISHING ALLOWED."

Without the experience of forgiving her enemies, Corrie's messages would have been hollow. Forgiveness, however, was not an emotion that happened once and then continued without interruption. Corrie struggled with other encounters, especially the nurse who was cruel to Betsie in the hospital barracks.

It was in 1954, ten years after this woman had spoken harshly to the dying Betsie. Corrie met the nurse in a friend's house, and at the moment of recognition she was seized with hatred. Ashamed that she was not practicing the very thing she taught, Corrie confessed her guilt and prayed, "Forgive me for my hatred, O Lord. Teach me to love my enemies."

Corrie was told that a group of young girls had been praying for the nurse for several months. It was the message Corrie needed to give her courage. She said, "When people pray for the salvation of someone, it indicates that God is working. He puts it in our hearts and minds to intercede, and what God begins He will complete."

As God worked through Corrie she led both the former guard and the hospital nurse to a knowledge of the saving grace of Jesus Christ.

Since Corrie often said, "The Lord has no problems, only plans," there was another surprise He had for her in Germany. She met the judge, the Sachbearbeiter who had been so good to them, the man who had taken the incriminating papers that had been found in the Beje and burned them in his stove. This man also accepted Jesus as Savior. Corrie wrote to friends in his town and asked them to visit him and take him to church. They tried several times, but never succeeded in finding him. Several months later Corrie found out that he had fallen into deep depression and committed suicide. After that, she began to emphasize the importance of follow-up work with a new believer.

Another prison guard, Carl, had been sentenced to sixteen years imprisonment in the jail at Vught, the very place where he had practiced his cruelties. Corrie was shown a letter from Carl, while she was in Germany, in which he said that he had accepted Jesus as Savior. After reading this, Corrie decided to request an amnesty for him from Queen Juliana. Before she wrote to her queen, however, she decided to go to Vught to see Carl.

She walked into the courtyard where she and Betsie had stood, trembling with the remembrance of the Dutchmen who were shot before their eyes. When she met Carl, he said to her, "How happy I am that my sins have been taken away."

For a moment Corrie had the same doubts so many of us have felt. Is forgiveness that simple? Here was a man who was part of the barbarism that caused many people to die. Was he really no longer guilty?

Corrie wrote: "It is an immutable law of God that man finds peace only when he is continually ready to forgive. Suddenly I see what I am doing. Carl's sins have been cast by Jesus into the depths of the sea. They are forgiven and forgotten—and I am trying to fish them up again!"

Corrie learned a lesson in Carl's cell. When Jesus requires that we love our enemies, He gives us the love He demands from us. We are channels of His love, not reservoirs. A reservoir can spring a leak, and all the love could be drained away. A channel provides the method for a continual flow from the ocean of God's love.

15

Tumbleweed

In the 1950s the world was trying to recover from its wounds; nations were struggling to rebuild. On the ideological front, World War II had a devastating impact on Christianity, both physically and morally; the alliance of Western democracies with the totalitarian Soviet Union was a great concern to many Christians.

Into the language of the day came a new term: *cold war,* describing the hostility between communist and anticommunist. The Soviets preached the doctrines of atheism and continued their drive for worldwide conquest.

In China, a new variety of Marxism was practiced by the communist leader, Mao Tse-tung. As the People's Republic of China was established Mao's government expelled all missionaries, liquidated church organizations, and subjected believers to intense persecution.

In Africa, Asia, and Latin America, the "theology of liberation," which was a so-called Christian variety of Marxism, appealed to revolutionary leaders.

Growing anticommunist sentiments began to develop in America, building to a crescendo in the 1960s.

However, as the level of religious persecution grew in communist Europe and China, the seeds were being planted for an accelerated worldwide Christian movement. It was in 1950 that Billy Graham brought together a talented team of believers to form the Billy Graham Evangelistic Association. One of this team, Cliff Barrows, had met Corrie in Switzerland at a Youth for Christ meeting in 1948. More than twenty years later, Corrie would impact the lives of Graham and his associates in a way they never would have dreamed of during those formative years of that far-reaching organization.

In Holland, a young, brash Dutchman was led into a dangerous ministry that took him behind the Iron Curtain with his Bibles and messages of hope. A pioneering missionary in this area, he became known as "Brother Andrew, God's smuggler." In later years, his ministry and Corrie's were joined in many ways.

During the same years, an evangelist with a fervor for revival was traveling the world with messages that stirred thousands to hear the Gospel of Jesus Christ. Dr. J. Edwin Orr's influence upon Corrie's life opened the doors for her in many areas of this hemisphere.

Tramping into this searching decade came this stocky Dutch woman, looking for places to tell her story. She was far from defeated, but she had surrendered. She wrote:

> When I was a prisoner of Adolf Hitler and his followers, I had to surrender completely against my will. During the time I was a prisoner I could not decide anything myself. I just had to obey. We have to obey somebody else—God. He is not a dictator, but a loving Father. There is no limit to what He will do for us and no end to His blessings, if we surrender to Him. Surrender is trusting God.

In one of her many photographs you may see a picture of tumbleweed. This is not exactly a work of art for posterity, but her caption says, "This is tumbleweed. It is being carried by the wind and leaves its seed everywhere. I was called a tumbleweed, because I was traveling all over the world, leaving the seed of the Gospel behind me."

As the tumbleweed was blown around the world, the doors were opened to receive her in many ways. Sometimes by careful planning, but more often by accident.

Phyllis Wildeson, the wife of a California minister, recalled that in 1950 Corrie had been invited to speak at a prayer meeting in Oakland, California. When the main speaker didn't show up, Corrie substituted. It was there that Corrie revealed her long-range plans. She said she was going to go around the world and tell her story and return to America every four years.

Also in California she was introduced to a group of Hollywood celebrities who were part of the Hollywood Christian group. When she arrived, she had just two dresses to her name. When she returned to her friend, Katie Cheney, in the East, she had six dresses. One of the movie celebrities had taken her shopping for clothes. Corrie said, "I never had a problem when I had a couple of dresses, now I have six dresses and six problems, because I have to make a decision."

Another time, her niece, Nolly ten Boom, accompanied her to America and told about a car ride they took in a mountainous area. A young man was driving rather carelessly along the winding road, with a wall of granite on one side and an abyss on the other. Corrie was sleeping in the backseat as she usually did between lectures, when suddenly the car went into a spin and came to an abrupt stop, heading in the opposite direction. Corrie opened her eyes and said to the driver, "You certainly keep the angels busy, John."

When Corrie felt the Lord was leading her into a certain area, she could be very insistent. While she was staying with Katie Cheney she found out that her friend had spent a vacation in Bermuda; when she returned home Katie had begun to pray that many people on that beautiful island would accept Jesus Christ. Corrie said, "Katie, I want you to open all the doors for me. God wants me to go to Bermuda."

Katie Cheney became a "can opener" to prepare the way for Corrie. Although she didn't have money for the plane trip, Corrie asked the Lord for guidance, and it became clear to her that He wanted her to go. Two or three days after she wrote people in Bermuda that she would come, checks arrived from people who knew nothing about the proposed trip.

During one week in Bermuda, Corrie had more than twenty speaking engagements. She talked at the Rotary Club, on radio stations, and in prisons. She wrote to Dr. Orr: "Never before have I experienced such a working of the Holy Spirit. People asked for the Gospel. In one of the prisons a kind of revival started, and later on it began outside of the prisons."

One Bermudan black man said: "I never knew there were real children of God among the white people, but since our prayer meeting I know better. God gave you a good training in your work among the feebleminded in Holland. Now you speak so simply that all of us can understand you."

In Bermuda, an island of natural beauty and friendly people, Corrie was taken to a store and urged to buy something for herself. In her mind she flashed back to the time when she was in Scheveningen, a gray, colorless prison where she was not even allowed the luxury of walking on the corridor runner.

Fresh from her spiritual triumph in Bermuda, Corrie returned to the States and went to Cleveland and Chicago. The meetings were poorly attended; her schedules and arrangements were confused. She missed connections and seemed to do the wrong thing at every turn.

How many of us would blame others for plans that sour? Corrie said, "I had often said to people, 'If there is a shadow somewhere in your past of which you do not like to be reminded, stop where you are and take it to God in prayer. Ask Him to retrace your steps with you to that dark spot.'"

So Corrie prayed, "Lord, go back with me to Chicago and Cleveland. What was wrong there?"

To Corrie the answer was clear, "Cleveland and Chicago, that was Corrie ten Boom without Me. Bermuda, that was Corrie with Me."

From Holland, to Germany, to America, and then around the world, God's tumbleweed bounced along, touching lives, growing as a spokeswoman for the Lord she served. She kept notes, wrote letters to friends, and began to write some of the "little books" (pronounced by Corrie *boooks*) that were preparatory to her career as a best-selling author.

In her extensive correspondence with Dr. Edwin Orr, we are able to trace her travels and spiritual impact. Before she left America to return to Germany, she wrote:

> I hope that, if the Lord tarries, I soon may come back to America and then work under your guidance. The first half year of 1951, I will work in West Germany. I am so happy about what you wrote about the religious awakening in America. If only God gave that to Germany! There is so much coldness in the churches. The theology is often so negative. . . . How wonderful that Hollywood people are entering Christian ministry! I knew that God was working there in a marvelous way.

Between trips, Corrie returned to Holland and arranged for the purchase of a new house, an extension of the ministry for hurting people. This house, called *Zonneduin,* was also in the beautiful area of Bloemendaal and became Corrie's home base during her travels. It was also the location for one of her most crushing disappointments, which resulted in another lesson in forgiveness.

On her sixtieth birthday Corrie was in Japan, a country for which she had a great burden, especially for the missionaries. While in Tokyo she wrote, "I see much work for me here. We need a good home where missionaries can live and have good care. Pray that God gives me the vision, wisdom, and money to do what is needed."

Fund-raising events, however, were not her style. In Japan, when Corrie spoke for a dinner where the people were asked to subscribe the amount they would give for the coming year, she gave a strong message in which she said that if they gave many dollars, but did not open their hearts to the fullness of the Holy Spirit, their works would be like hay and stubble. It would have been interesting to see the face of the minister who headed that fund raiser!

In Japan she wrote:

> Japan is a very heathen country. Many so-called Christians are using their Buddhism as a kind of Christianity. Liberalism has ruined the churches. With "American oppression" leaving, much Christianity disappeared. The Japanese are proud of their wisdom of the wise. Jesus, Lord of all, the longing for His coming again, the Holy Spirit, these are often strange truths for many Japanese. God uses me much to encourage missionaries. What sterling silver people they are, but many are discouraged.

She had the support of many people around the world, praying for her. However, at the age of sixty, sleeping in different beds, eating different food every day, constantly on the move, she said, "God does the miracle that although I work very hard, I am not tired."

While in Japan, another worldwide traveler in God's work, Dr. Edwin Orr, wrote to her urging her to come to South Africa. He said that her message of forgiveness was greatly needed there.

Travels with Corrie sound like the schedule of a transcontinental airline pilot. She wanted very much to join Dr. Orr in South Africa, but she wrote, "In January and February I expect to be in Formosa, in March and April in Australia and New Zealand, part of April and May in South Africa, and in Palestine and Spain in June. All this, of course God willing."

Corrie said that she "longed for a real revival," and Dr. Orr admonished her, "Schedules are the enemy of revival. I do not see how a revivalist can plan a revival within certain limits any more than a physician can plan the duration of a cure. But when the revival breaks. . . ."

What constitutes a revival? If numbers are significant, certainly there was a revival in South Africa in 1952. Among the students, there were more than ten thousand in high school and colleges who professed decisions for Christ in those meetings.

In airports, on trains, scribbled in notebooks in her cramped, almost illegible writing, Corrie kept writing. Her books, like her sermons, were simple, but filled with a depth of understanding. Germany, particularly, began to open to her as a result of her booklet *Amazing Love.* She said that she had more invitations than she could cover. Germany took every inch of her, spiritually and physically. She saw that modern heathenism and demonism were prevalent and that cults dating back to the middle ages sprang up in the villages. She deplored the theologians who were involved in Bible criticism but ignored the deep spiritual needs of their people. According to Corrie, the German ministers often taught with a "dark face and a lifted finger." With her irrepressible twinkle and unexpected humor, she must have been a refreshing change. "I am glad God made me to bring a joyful message," she said.

Corrie, the independent woman—Corrie, the lone piece of tumbleweed, directed by the wind of the Lord—was soon to become a team player. The Revival Fellowship Team, under the direction of evangelist Edwin Orr and associated with the International Council of Christian Leadership of Washington, whose president was Princess Wilhelmina, prepared for a major campaign in Australia and New Zealand. Dr. Orr, recalling those days, twenty-eight years later, said that Corrie was a great team player and that although he was twenty years younger, Corrie had great respect for his leadership. One story he told was about Corrie's experience in the Brethren Assembly: The Brethren would not have a woman speak in their church meetings, under the scriptural admonition that women should keep silent in the churches. To circumvent this ruling the announcement was made: "As you know, our dear sister Corrie ten Boom will be speaking for a whole week to the sisters of the assembly. If any of the brethren would like to know what the sisters are being told, they are heartily welcome to attend."

Throughout her life, Corrie had men with strong spiritual gifts who influenced and directed her. For months Corrie and Dr. Orr worked together or individually, speaking in Australia and New Zealand. After a grueling schedule, anyone else might need a vacation; but Corrie went to India. In the land of temples and poverty, Corrie thought her work was a "grand adventure." Although the climate made her lazy, she also found India fascinating. She wrote to Edwin Orr and said, "I know that there is work for you here. How India needs your message. . . . I hope to meet you somewhere in India, Boss."

Corrie may have been "lazy" in her mind, but she also experienced the most crowded meetings of her speaking career to date. Thousands came to hear her, and they did not expect short sermons; Corrie could talk as long as she wished. She said that India was the happiest time of her life, as far as she could remember.

For a woman who had accepted Jesus as her Savior when she was five years old, it is surprising to discover that she was baptized at the age of sixty-six in a church in India. She wrote, "It was the most unusual baptismal service they ever saw. I gave the sermon myself."

As Corrie continued around the world: from India to Borneo, Korea, Japan, Formosa, Hong Kong, Vietnam, Israel, Europe, her intensity of purpose seemed to pick up momentum. She said, "I have prayed the Lord will give me ten new evangelistic sermons and ten revival sermons. I know that He will do it. I have a strong sense of being just in the beginning and in training for a greater ministry." She wrote this in 1958.

During this era, Corrie would return to her home in Zonneduin for a time of writing and visiting. During the Australian and New Zealand work with the Revival Fellowship Team, she had sent as much money as she could for the upkeep of the Holland home. Dr. Orr had a "check in his spirit," which was his way of saying that he was uneasy about Corrie sending this money to Holland. On one journey home she was abruptly dispossessed, in a manner that was not very gracious. It was one of the most difficult blows of her life. She did not speak of it often, except that in later years, when she was talking about forgiveness, she related to a friend this story of the unceremonious manner in which she was informed that her room was no longer available. He asked, "Have you forgiven them?"

"Of course I have. But I've kept all the letters about what they did to me. It's all down in black and white."

"Corrie, the Lord said to forgive and forget. You need to burn all of these black and whites."

Another blow came when the publisher in Holland refused her book *Not Good if Detached.* He told her that she was influenced by the Anglo-Saxons. (An unusual comment.) Although Corrie stated frequently that she was a Dutch woman through and through, she also began to feel that she was growing away from Holland as she became more of a citizen of the world.

Most writers have sacred little corners where they compose their deathless prose or poetry. They have favorite typewriters, pencils, or colors of papers. Their "inspiration" must have a particular setting or environment. Corrie shared her writing techniques while she was in England in 1959. "The Lord led me to write a new book about experiences in soul winning and the second part about the more victorious life, normal life for a Christian. I wrote it waiting in traffic jams, in bus stations, and also often sitting in trains or buses or planes. I have never understood how it is possible when the Lord inspires you to write a book when you have no quietness. Will you pray for that book? First I thought to call it *Operation Paratroopers,* but that was, I think, a little bit too military."

As her fame grew, Corrie faced the age-old danger of pride. Many Christians who have been placed in positions of prominence quickly lose their sense of God power and adopt the attitude of me power. Corrie wrote to Dr. Orr:

> Will you pray always for me that people will not see Corrie ten Boom, but the Lord, when I speak?
>
> I worked in Germany with unusual blessings. Never have I worked so intensely, but it almost did hurt my health. To have an abundance of food and traveling through a hungry crowd is a joy that the disciples knew at the miracle of the multiplication of the loaves. I received it from the Lord's hand and passed it on. I just could not stop, even when I got the flu. I had to learn that I am no longer sixteen years old.

However, in the next breath she announced her plans for the coming months: Switzerland, Denmark, a week in Holland with the "old Queen," Israel, India, and Africa.

During the journeys of that first decade of tramping for the Lord, Corrie had the constant strain of leaving the family and friends she loved. When she returned to Holland, she spent as much time with her beloved "big sister," Nollie, as she could. When Nollie died in 1953, Corrie was in Switzerland with her nephew, Nollie's youngest son, Peter. She returned to Holland in time for the burial services, but left soon afterwards, sure that she had overcome her sorrow and that her personal ministry would continue strong as ever. But this was not true; the following months seemed dry and fruitless. Corrie would get discouraged easily.

A year later Corrie returned to Haarlem and slipped outside a telephone booth, severely injuring her hip. She was ordered to stay in bed until she was healed, and since she was due back in Germany for a student conference, she became very impatient.

One morning she asked her friends, "Isn't there a Christian around here who has the gift of healing?"

They called a man to come and see Corrie, and the first question he asked was one she knew well, for she had posed that question to others. "Corrie, are there unrepented sins in your life?"

Corrie knew she had been impatient and had demanded a lot from her nurse and friends; she repented of these sins of attitude. The man prayed with her and laid his hands on her in the name of Jesus. At that moment something happened which Corrie never forgot.

It had been a year since Nollie had died. Although she thought she had surrendered her sorrow to the Lord, deep in her heart she was mourning. Nollie's death had left Corrie with a feeling of insecurity and unhappiness, which had kept her from doing her best work. But when this man prayed, she described a stream of power that went through her. Her mourning left and never came back, but she also felt the presence of the Lord Jesus and a great peace and joy that was so intense that she prayed, "Not more, Lord, not more, my heart could break for joy."

In ten days she left for Germany, leaning on a walking stick, but with more strength than the doctors could have imagined.

Corrie knew that Jesus said, "You will receive power after the Holy Spirit has come upon you." That is what happened to her. God knew that in Germany she had to fight face to face with demonic powers, and now she had power as never before. It was after this that her ministry in Germany exploded.

Corrie, raised in the Dutch Reformed Church, influenced by her Calvinist father, was not prone to emotionalism. Yet this, and other experiences in later years, could label her as *charismatic*. However, her life and ministry defy labels, and those who would place her in categories soon find themselves shrugging off any doctrinal differences because of the results of her ministry.

She said, "Must I give this experience a name? Some people call it the baptism of the Holy Spirit. Others call it the second blessing. I don't try to give it a name. It was the beginning of a new spiritual blessing that brought me into a deeper experience with the Lord and a greater sense of His abiding presence."

Corrie never felt that she had "arrived" in her spiritual knowledge. She was always learning, always seeking to know more of God's will for her. It was this sense of childish wonder that kept her young as she aged, strong in her weakness.

16

Walking in the Light

"How dark are the clouds in the world! It is good to know the secret of God's plan. He has no problems, only plans."

Corrie repeated those words around the world and constantly needed to remind herself of their truth. In the turbulent times of the 1960s, with unrest among the students of the world, campus riots, the war in Vietnam, and the increase in evangelical fervor, Corrie began to add momentum to her ministry as time added years to her age.

She was in England, speaking at a Bible school for young women, when God answered her prayers for a traveling companion, a team-mate, to accompany her around the world. Conny van Hoogstraten became the first of three young women who came into Corrie's life at the right moment. Conny had been in a Japanese prison camp for three years, studied history at the University of Amsterdam, and was a fun-loving Dutch girl.

For Conny, thirty-one years old, the first few months with Corrie, sixty-eight years old, were lived at a dizzy pace. Corrie said that the Lord had shown her four countries to visit: Denmark, Austria, Israel, and India. "Buy our tickets to Tel Aviv, Conny. I have the money for the plane that far."

When Conny discovered from the travel office that a visa to Israel was only possible if tickets were purchased to another place outside Israel, Corrie said, "Then order the tickets to Calcutta."

"Do we have the money?" asked Conny, still untried in her employer's faith walk.

"No, not yet, but don't forget, God is our treasurer. He has the cattle on a thousand hills, and He will perhaps sell some cows and give us the money. Our work is His business, and He always provides the money just in time."

When the tickets arrived, the money was there.

When you met Corrie, you didn't forget her. Some people reacted to her with a feeling of inadequacy. However, as Conny soon discovered, working closely with another human being, especially one who was used to making her own arrangements and schedules, was a challenge in relationships.

First, the pace of travel, meetings, and arrangements was hectic for the girl just out of a quiet English Bible school. Someone told Conny, "If you are going to work with Corrie ten Boom, you might be a few miles away from the Taj Mahal and never have time to visit it." That was right. In New Delhi, only a short distance from one of the wonders of the world, she never saw it.

Conny knew that the Lord had called her to be Corrie's companion, but she believed that Corrie lived on a different spiritual level. She was, however, content in her new role, as long as she could remain polite to Corrie. Africa changed that attitude and the relationship.

They went to Uganda, and an African brother, William Nagenda, asked a bold, and probing question: "Do you walk in the light together?" Both Conny and Corrie responded emphatically, "We do!"

It is a humbling experience to admit to carrying resentment against a spiritual superior. Conny remembered the suitcase episode. Their luggage was overweight on one of their trips, and Corrie decided to do something about it. She ransacked her own suitcase, giving some things away and sending other possessions to Holland. Then she proceeded to take Conny's personal possessions out of her bag and sort them out in the same way. Conny went into the bathroom where she could be alone, and prayed, "Lord, forgive me my anger; take it away."

Another time, when they were in India, Corrie had planned the winter schedule in the coldest countries and the summer schedule

in the hottest areas. Conny resented this lack of consideration.

These, and other hidden differences, were stirring within Conny when she was confronted by this question of "walking in the light." The Bible says, "But if we walk in the light, as he is in the light, we have fellowship with one another, and the blood of Jesus, his Son, purifies us from every sin" (1 John 1:7 NIV).

Conny went to William Nagenda and told him she couldn't confess her sins of resentment to Corrie; she would feel so humiliated. He gave her advice that altered Corrie's relationships with her close companions and associates. He said, "You can, Conny. Go in the strength of the Lord."

Conny confessed her sins to Corrie and asked forgiveness. Corrie wrote in her diary, "Looking at her, I saw how I had failed. I am like an old soldier, trained in a rugged school. I had expected her to have the same reaction as mine in difficult experiences."

She also asked Conny for forgiveness—forgiveness for provoking her to resentment, for demanding too much from her.

The old woman, a seasoned "Tramp for the Lord," and the young student "walked in the light," and didn't wait for resentments to shake their relationship.

Life with Corrie was an adventure in laughter, hardship, and surprises. On one trip in New York, it was necessary for Corrie and Conny to take a helicopter between meeting places. They left their luggage behind, which was an unfortunate decision, because Conny became very airsick. Corrie helped her take off her soiled dress and gave her a coat to wear. When they arrived, without their luggage, in the small town where Corrie was to speak, poor Conny had only a heavy coat, and Corrie, in her usual direct manner said, "We will find pajamas for me and a dress for you." There were only five stores in the town, and the first four had no pajamas large enough for Corrie. Finally, at the fifth store, Corrie said to the astounded clerk, "I have prayed about these pajamas, and the Lord told me that you have them." She was shown a pair of pajamas that fit perfectly, and Conny found a sale on dresses and bought one for two dollars. Conny said she would wear the dress, and the clerk asked if she could wrap her old one. "No thank you, I didn't have a dress on when I came in." The saleswoman replied, "I have worked in this shop for eighteen years, but I have never had a customer before who came here without a dress on, nor anyone who prayed for the exact size of pajamas."

Corrie's life was prayer. It didn't matter whether it was a plane ticket, a parking place, or pajamas, she asked the Lord and trusted in His answers.

When Betsie envisioned a ministry that would take them around the world, telling of God's love and forgiveness, she never dreamed of motion pictures as a vehicle. The ten Booms were brought up in an atmosphere that did not condone movies. However, in 1960 the first seed of this method of communication was planted in Corrie's mind. A woman from West Pakistan, an editor of a magazine expressing the views of the student Christian movement of that country, wrote Corrie that she had asked the publisher of Corrie's book *A Prisoner and Yet*, a small book published by Christian Literature Crusade in 1954, if she could obtain the film rights to this story. She wrote Corrie, "I feel very strongly that the experiences and experiments of faith that are presented in your book must get across to more people, and a film is the best medium for such a venture."

A film? Corrie was tempted, but something held her back from this venture. Perhaps she was beginning to envision an outreach that was larger than the few hundred people who came out to hear her in those days. She wrote, "In Switzerland I met Billy Graham. He looked fine. He is willing to write the foreword in my next book." (Almost twenty years later, Billy Graham did write that foreword, but it was in a book about Corrie, not one she wrote herself.)

Corrie and Conny, the old trooper and the young scholar, were a traveling, praying, speaking team. It was during the seething sixties that Corrie became more burdened for the nation of Israel. She found working in the land for which she had prayed daily all of her life was a difficult task. She was sad to find that many Jews equated Christianity with Hitlerism, which was a double wound to her sensitivities. She wrote, "It is difficult for a Hebrew Christian to testify boldly. Pray that Conny and I may be used to give the Christians a new vision of the victorious life. After all, Jesus had said, 'Indeed, in the world you will have tribulation, but be of good cheer! I have overcome the world.' "

The Israelis made a list of "righteous gentiles," which is the name they gave to non-Jews who had given their lives and time to save the Jewish people. Corrie discovered that her name was on that list, and doors began to open in a country that was not too receptive to Christian missionaries. In one meeting she was introduced by a rabbi who said, "Now Corrie ten Boom will tell us about her greatest friend, the Jew Jesus."

When she spoke, she said that Jesus, from His human side, was the Messiah of Israel, born of the Jewish virgin, Mary; from His divine side, He is the Son of God. Some Jews began to get up and leave the meeting, but others present reprimanded them and told them to sit down and listen to what she had to say.

A doctor said after that meeting, "When I hear Corrie ten Boom tell about the joy and security she had from her Jesus, even in such difficult circumstances, and what love He had given her for her enemies, I almost envy her and get a longing to know the Lord Jesus more intimately."

One day Corrie was being interviewed for the *Jerusalem Post;* she sensed that she was facing an antagonistic reporter. As she was trying to answer his questions she saw an old retired missionary enter the hall of the Jerusalem YMCA, glance at Corrie and the reporter, go to a corner in the room, sit down, and pray. Corrie said, "When people pray, the enemy hasn't much chance to come in between while the Holy Spirit works."

The reporter asked, "Why do you love the Jews?"

She answered, "There are three reasons. First, I have to thank you Jews for two great blessings in my life, a Book, bursting with good news: the Tanach, Old Testament, and the fulfillment of the Tanach, the New Testament, written by Jews. Only Luke was not a Jew, but converted by a Jew.

"Second, my greatest friend and Savior, who is my security and joy in all circumstances, was a Jew.

"Third, my family and I have sacrificed our lives for your people. Three of them died for your sake, and I suffered much and almost lost my life for your people. Such an experience brings much love in one's heart. The love for you Jews is in my blood, since my grandfather prayed for the peace of Jerusalem."

The article that was published in the *Jerusalem Post* was very sympathetic. Corrie said, "Was it because of the interviewer or tact and love from my side? No, the old missionary who prayed in the corner of that hall was the reason."

For seven years Conny helped Corrie on and off airplanes, trains, camels, rickshaws, and platforms. The indefatigable old woman carried one message, with new illustrations, wherever there was a listening ear and sometimes when the ears seemed closed.

In Russia, Corrie and Conny went into a hotel dining room for breakfast and handed their room key to a woman sitting in the hallway, which was the requirement in the hotel. Whenever Corrie saw an outstretched hand it was an invitation for a tract. The woman pushed the salvation message away, and looked furtively down the hall. Corrie and Conny walked into the elevator, and Corrie suddenly prayed, "Lord, I claim the soul of this woman for eternity. I cannot reach her, but You can. Would You please save her?"

"Corrie, can we really claim her for the Lord?"

Corrie, who was never accused of thinking small, then prayed, "Lord, I claim all of Russia for Jesus. Your Word says the earth and the fulness thereof is the Lord's, and that includes Russia as well. I do not understand it, but I do claim it."

After breakfast, they returned to their room, and there was a knock on the door. It was the woman who kept the keys. She poured out a stream of Russian words, pointing to Corrie's purse. Conny said, "She wants to have that tract." Corrie fished out the tract, gave it to her, and she left, beaming all over.

In the latter part of 1964, Corrie became severely ill with hepatitis, and the doctor ordered her to take a year's sabbatical leave. Corrie prayed for a place of quiet and rest and was led to Uganda and the home of Harry and Evelyn Campbell, Christian friends who ran a chain of bookstores in that troubled country. Their beautiful home was located by a lake, with palm-shaded lawns and profuse poinsettia shrubs.

Harry Campbell said, "After some weeks of rest and special diet prepared by my wife, Corrie started to recover slowly. She didn't like any fuss being made over her. When she got attacks of pain, she would slip away to her room and pray, and in an amazing way the Lord touched her."

Corrie would stroll in the garden in the cool of the evening, admiring the beautiful birds, such as the crested cranes, and laughing at the red-tailed monkeys. Soon she became restless, "May I speak somewhere, Harry?" she would ask. The Campbells allowed her to talk to their bookshop staff in Kampala. Corrie spoke to the group, using her famous flashlight filled with pieces of rags. When she put the first battery in, it was an indication of accepting Jesus into your life. Then she would press the button, but the flashlight wouldn't work.

"What is this?" she would ask in mock dismay; and then she would begin to pull out rags and name each piece with a different sin. "This one is pride, this one envy, and here is the love of money. When they are removed and replaced with the Holy Spirit, the light is able to shine."

The Africans loved the illustration in 1965, and sophisticated Americans applauded the same illustration in 1975. Simplistic? Perhaps.

Corrie was seventy-two, sick, old, and impatient. She wrote, "Conny and my working together as a team is a daily blessing. Although I work part-time in prisons and churches, I am longing for the time that I may go on 100 percent."

The next year Corrie and Conny worked behind the Iron Curtain for two months. They went to Russia, Hungary, Czechoslovakia, and Poland, encouraging believers in Christ. It was not an easy time, but Corrie wrote, "It was such a joy to tell the brothers and sisters in Christ in Eastern Europe of the fellowship in prayer they have with Christians in other countries. What a privilege it was to be able to tell them that Jesus is Victor and that the whole world is His."

One time she was warned by a very apprehensive woman, "Be sure you do not tell dangerous things to me. The communists are listening. Everywhere they have their secret microphones."

Corrie saw that the woman was so frightened it would have been impossible to talk to her about the Lord, so she prayed for wisdom. Then her eyes twinkled, and she preached a little sermon, hoping that hidden microphones would be channeled to receptive ears.

"Do you know that your soul is very precious in God's eyes? There is an ocean of God's love available through Jesus Christ. Bring your problems to Him who has said: 'Come to me, all who are heavy laden, and I will give you rest.'

"He will give you peace and joy when you surrender all to Him. He loves you."

Corrie grasped the opportunity, whatever her circumstances.

The year of her Iron Curtain visits also saw Corrie in America again, this time spending some time with friends in Colorado Springs, writing her biography, which was published in Dutch under the title of *In Hem Geborgen* and in German under the title, *In Ihm Geborgen.* How long did it take? A few months, perhaps, as her usual race with God's time clock forced her on. She wrote her friend Brother Andrew, in Holland, that the Lord had promised her ten more years on the mission field.

It was just a little more than ten years later that she settled down in America and moved into a beautiful house in California. Her days of being a missionary without a permanent place of residence were over. Coincidence? Perhaps.

Meanwhile, Corrie had a home in Holland, an apartment in Soestdijk, near the royal palace, that a dear friend, Baroness Elisabeth van Heemstra, loaned her as home base between journeys. For the first time in twenty years, Corrie stayed in Holland for almost six months. She thought, in fact, that the luxurious flat, with its view of Dutch skies, trees, and flowers, would be her home for the rest of her life. However, anyone who feels too old for change should grab the coattails of Corrie, for she couldn't settle down in comfort and luxury. First, there was a new companion to find. Conny fell in love with Lykle Hoogerzeil and began to prepare for a new ministry with her missionary husband.

Conny was married for only a year and a half before she became critically ill. Corrie went to Conny and said to her, "Two things can happen: The Lord can heal you, or the Lord will take you to heaven, so you must prepare."

When Conny was dying, her husband sat beside her bedside and said, "Give me your hand, when the Lord takes it, I will release you." Corrie preached at Conny's funeral.

Corrie was not to stay in Holland. She said, "I know that I am not yet called to stay here. Every Christian must try to find the special place where he can be used and others cannot. For me there are many such places and countries. So on I go, in the strength of the Lord."

Where next? Holland had its pleasant flat near the palace of the queen. America had many homes where Corrie would be treated like royalty. Where next, Lord? Vietnam? Certainly not, Corrie! When there are younger people, stronger souls, why would God want to send an old Dutch woman to the bloody battlefields of Southeast Asia?

Soldier, soldier, fighting in the world's great strife,
On yourself relying, battling for your life.
Trust yourself no longer,
Trust in Christ, He's stronger!
You can all things, all things, do
Through Christ who strengthens you.

Part IV

Crossing Time
and Space

Each year Corrie confronted more opportunities and more challenges. She longed to work behind the Iron Curtain, but many times her visa was refused. However, she wrote, "I'm knocked down, but not knocked out! Is it not a joy to know that our times are in God's hands?"

Corrie, citizen of the world, ambassador to young and old, plunged into projects and situations where more cautious souls would wait and evaluate all the consequences before venturing. She began to see a picture of the times as one of extremes. She said, "Everywhere in the world you see that the iniquities increase, but also the Holy Spirit transforms and equips people with power from on high."

Bring out the trumpets; sound the clarion call. Corrie is leading the battalion.

She warned, "We are approaching the great end battle, which will have its climax in the victory of the King of kings, Jesus Christ. The Antichrist is marching on and does his utmost, and the devil knows that his time is short.

"What a privilege we have above the world around us, that we know the secret of God's plan.

"Even when the battle gets severe, we stand on victory ground, for those who are with us are stronger than those who are against us."

17

Passport for a Warrior

Corrie was influenced by strong men of faith, visionaries with ideas and plans that were bold and challenging. Age was inconsequential; it was dedication to the Lord that Corrie sought. From these spiritual and intellectual associations developed some unusual teamwork.

One of these men was Andrew van der Byl, a teammate thirty years younger, but dedicated to reaching the world for Christ, just like Corrie. Known as Brother Andrew, this wiry Dutchman, zealous in a ministry that smuggled thousands of Bibles behind the Iron and Bamboo Curtains, was a more likely adventurer for a mission as dangerous as Vietnam during the height of a bloody conflict, than an old woman of seventy-five. But Corrie wanted to talk to the GIs, and she was no stranger to hardship. So she went to Vietnam with Brother Andrew.

Corrie was so thrifty that she would save leftovers from the airline meals, to be taken out and eaten later. Brother Andrew said, "She would turn a cent over until it was all worn out." When they arrived in Saigon, she stored her briefcase under the bed and took it out a day later to use her notes for a talk. The inside was crawling with black ants; that was the last time she stashed away food in the tropics.

As they traveled to Vietnam, Andrew was reading a newspaper and came across the military expression "to search and destroy." He was saddened, knowing that they were going in service for the Lord to win souls for Him, "Corrie, look at this phrase. Tell me what you think."

"Andrew, I think of the words of Jesus, 'I came to seek and to save that which was lost.' "

Corrie's diary reflected the strain of that trip. She wrote:

> Yesterday I arrived here. The journey in the aircraft was terrible. We took a route over the water, because there is less danger there of being shot at. When I got into the aircraft, I was already tired . . . after two hours I could hardly stand it. At the moment I feel very old. It is just as if I have crossed the border of my physical abilities. At that time, you're very dependent upon the Lord. When you are weak, then He is strong.
>
> I was reminded how someone once prayed in a meeting, "Lord, make us all as weak as Corrie ten Boom." When I got out of the aircraft, everything was going around. A couple of missionaries came . . . I was so finished I hardly recognized anyone.

Corrie was not immune to self-pity. She began to think that the work of reaching the world (especially in Vietnam) was too heavy for her. Then she wrote:

> I look at the faces around me, and experience deep sympathy. I know I have work for the kingdom of God. After what He did for me on the cross, then I am happy that I can suffer a little. I open my Bible and read John 7:37. I am thirsty. . . . I am thirsty for forgiveness, for power. That is what I lack. But Jesus is the answer. I lay my weak hand in Jesus' strong hand. And then when I get into the aircraft again, there is no self-pity anymore, only joy . . . streams of living water will flow from inside me if I am connected up with the source."

The Vietnam War was a grueling, nasty conflict. In America, people were divided about the very reasons for the United States'

involvement in Southeast Asia. The communist world was foment-
ing this dissension, as well as sanctioning Vietcong atrocities.
Morale among the American GI's was low. Corrie was given special
transportation by the army so that she could go places where she
could minister.

One time she almost got to the front line in a Jeep. She bounced
along over some back road, with a young sergeant, apparently oblivious to his precious passenger, taking her so close to the battlefield that they could hear the shooting. She wrote, "The soldiers
were very happy that I came, because the only women they saw
around there were prostitutes. But here comes an old lady from
Holland to the battle line, and they thought that was great. I over-
heard one of the boys say, 'She has the same smile as my grandmother.' "

Wherever Corrie went, she took pictures. The photography may
not have been superb, but her captions became detailed stories. In
Vietnam she described a village church where she held a Bible
study. The people in this village were going to be killed by the
Vietcong, because they were Christians. One day the Vietcong came
and surrounded the village. One man, a Christian by the name of
Sao, told all of the villagers to get into the church and pray, asking
the Lord to protect them. As the hours passed, nothing happened.
The people prayed. Two days passed, and the enemy soldiers left.
Later, a Vietcong soldier was wounded, and the missionary doctor
in the village treated him. He asked him why the Vietcong had not
attacked. "We were planning to kill all of you," the man answered,
"but we didn't dare when we saw the big army in white uniforms
surrounding the village."

Corrie said, "A great army of angels came to surround the village,
and the enemy saw them. The funny part is that it was not the
Christians, who, according to Scripture, believed that the angels
were around them, but the enemy who had never heard about
angels!"

Sao, a Vietnamese who loved the Lord, was a courageous friend
of Corrie's. He traveled through the mountains of Vietnam, settling
down for a time with a tribe that was pagan, living and working
with them. He brought them a message from the Scriptures at night.
Sao told Corrie about a time when he thought he was dying. All his
family and friends stood around him, anticipating his death. But Sao
had a vision; he arrived in heaven with a friend, who was shown

to a beautiful home. Then he noticed a house that was under construction, and someone told him, "Sao, that is your home, but it's not quite finished; and besides, your feet are dirty." Sao was sad, because his friend was allowed to stay in heaven, and he had to return.

When he became conscious, the first thing he wanted was a basin to wash his feet. Everybody thought he was delirious. He said, "My feet are too dirty for heaven, but my friend is there and has a beautiful home." It was discovered later that his friend had died that very day.

The Vietcong hated Sao, because he led so many people to the Lord. He told Corrie, "I would not mind to die as a martyr for the Lord Jesus Christ."

"Sao, your home has not been finished yet, and your feet are still dirty. It is necessary that you still walk from one tribe to the other with your dirty feet. You have to live for the Lord before you may die for Him."

Corrie worked with Sao, giving Bible lessons for natives from the mountain tribes. They were enrapt listeners to this old lady who had traveled so far just to talk with them. When she left one tribe, Sao gave her a gift and a title. She very much appreciated this gesture. She told this poor mountain tribe, people living on a bare subsistence diet, with few possessions, "I am going to leave now. I sure hope that you will pray for me once in a while. I'll pray for you."

Sao came forward, handed her a copper bracelet, and said in beautiful English, "Double old grandmother, would you please communicate the thanksgiving from this tribe to your tribe for allowing you to come here?"

Corrie wrote, "Well, it's nice to be called double old grandmother when you're only seventy-five years old." For them it is an honor to be old, and they flattered her with the greatest compliment they could create.

Sao said, "We want to make a covenant with you. You now belong to our tribe, and we will remain united through our prayers."

One of the projects that Brother Andrew and Corrie had in Vietnam was to ransom children from slavery. When a Vietnamese ran into debt and was unable to pay, he would sell his children as servants. Andrew and Corrie found the funds to buy many of these children and have them placed in responsible Christian orphanages.

One time she told of a pastor who arrived at the orphanage with five children. He said, "My whole church had been murdered, and only the children and I had a chance to hide. Can they stay at the orphanage, and may I work here, too?"

The Vietcong killed Christians by burying them alive.

Corrie could have picked a rocking chair, instead she chose a battlefield.

However even warriors need a home base. In twenty years of tramping over the world, Corrie had many homes, but never a place she thought she would stay, until 1967. It was then that she shifted into a new phase. When Baroness van Heemstra, a close friend and a missionary in Jerusalem, gave Corrie the use of her flat, near the palace of the Queen, the Baroness said, "God used Tante Corrie as my teacher without her ever knowing it. It was not so much her spoken messages that I needed, but rather the sweet example of her practical daily life."

It was to this beautiful apartment that an unsophisticated, pretty young Dutch girl by the name of Ellen de Kroon went one beautiful summer day, to meet the legendary Corrie ten Boom. Ellen was a little in awe, going to a home near the Queen's palace. The meeting between the old warrior and the young nurse, who had been a Christian for only three years, was destined to develop into another working team that took them from the depths of Siberia to the heights of Hollywood. Ellen, who had never been out of Europe, who couldn't speak English, who never learned to drive a car or use a typewriter, discovered that when God chooses someone for a task, He equips her, also. Ellen thought of all the negative reasons why she was not fit to be Corrie's traveling companion and assistant. As she wrote in her own book, *My Years with Corrie:* "I will never forget what Corrie said next. It was so typical of her. Her face was bright, her eyes sparkling. 'Ellen, I'm happy you know it. You cannot do it, but God can do it through you.' "

It was soon evident that Ellen was the right person at the right time. Ellen had been trained as a nurse, and her skills were soon put to use. Corrie was in a serious car accident.

In a letter she later wrote to Brother Andrew, Corrie told about this accident and what she thought were the reasons for it.

> I want to tell about the circumstances I was involved in
> when I was in this accident. There were three messages that
> I'd made for transworld radio. Someone had asked me to

say something about victory over demons. The first message was, "Are We Powerless Against Demons . . . No!" The message was about the power of Jesus' blood and the authority of His Name. I was to give it that day, and then they were to send it to Monte Carlo and reach many all over the world, at least those who understood Dutch. Then I had the accident. I believe the devil was not happy with that message, and he tried to knock me out through that car accident. I was, indeed, knocked out, but through a miracle my life was spared. My arm was broken, but it was so close to my head that the combs which I wore in my hair were broken. How easily that could have touched my brain. But the Lord spared my life and allowed me a little bit of suffering, so I would learn a great deal. If a class in life's school is difficult, the Lord Jesus is standing in front of the class, and you learn a lot.

During the course of the operation and afterwards, the old, well-known hymns, such as "Safe in Jesus' Arms," "You Hold Both My Hands," were a help to me. It was as if the great truths of the Bible gave me a happiness I never had before . . . it was a very blessed time.

Sometimes I expected a direct miracle of healing and became rather despondent about this. Then I understood; God never makes mistakes. I had a very full program in Germany and Israel; instead of that I had to lie on my back for months. But what an opportunity to talk to the Lord. I learned so much, and repeatedly others, as well as myself, received prophecy that the work would not decrease, but maybe it would be a little different. But I know that Israel, Vietnam, and Russia are where the Lord wants to use me.

Ben Hoekendijk, a Dutch evangelist, recalled visiting Tante Corrie in the hospital and seeing her lying there, beaming and fully relaxed. She said to him, "The sickness is not from God, but from the enemy. That I lie here is from the Lord, because some in the hospital have found their salvation already."

Corrie was not all relaxation in the hospital; she was an impatient hospital patient, with so much she wanted to do and no right arm to do it. Since she couldn't write, it was probably during this time that she learned to dictate her messages and thoughts, which for many writers is not an easy skill.

On the day Ellen was to pick her up and take her home, the weather was very bad and the streets were icy. She had to navigate a Volkswagen on the narrow, bending roads through the Dutch villages. On one curve, her car went into a spin and smashed into a cement wall, a total wreck from which Ellen emerged with keys dangling from one hand and Corrie's suitcase in the other. She suffered a concussion and severe bruises, and when Corrie was finally transported home, there were two patients in the apartment.

It was during this time of recuperation that Corrie and Ellen established their deep friendship and the pattern for their working together. Routine was: coffee at 11:00 A.M. and a cup of tea with a biscuit at 3:00 P.M., take times during the day to read a book aloud or share some thoughts and pray. Ellen learned so much about the woman who was to shape her life in the next few years.

Ellen learned to know Corrie as a human being, filled with good traits and flaws. She began to understand the great determination of her employer. After the cast was off Corrie's arm, she was unable to use her right hand. At first she became discouraged, because she had so many ideas she wanted to put down on paper. However, she turned discouragement into action. She went to a bookstore and purchased a first-grade writing tablet, and began to copy her ABCs with her left hand. She also began to use a tape recorder, which was a new technique. She worked with weights and exercised her fingers. She refused to give in to inactivity.

Ellen and Corrie both had keen senses of humor, which is important in a close working relationship. The story is told about the time Ellen served soup, but forgot to put spoons on the table. Corrie said, "Ellen, eating soup with a fork is like kissing. You never get enough."

As they both became stronger, it was clear that the comfortable life in the beautiful little apartment was not where Corrie was going to snuggle in, tinker with her clocks, and knit. First, she needed another car. Ellen soon learned that Corrie always paid cash for a purchase, since she believed that it was easier to know God's will if she did. If she wanted something and she didn't have the money, she knew it wasn't for her. However, if the money came just in time for the purchase, then she knew it was God's will. This life of faith was new to Ellen, but it soon added a dimension to her living that transported the fun-loving blond Dutch girl into palaces and prisons.

18

In Palaces and Prisons

"Living in a sick and dangerous world as we do, we have a responsibility. Who will overcome the world? He who believes that Jesus is the Son of God. Our responsibility is to spread God's Word everywhere we go, so that more people will be numbered in God's family."

These are Corrie's words, and she acted upon them. Spreading God's Word has no regard for race, social position, or living conditions. Corrie saw people as individuals with a need to know Jesus Christ; their background was inconsequential.

In the late 1960s, the hippies, vagabonds, and shabbily dressed visitors caused some neighbors to look askance at the old woman who lived in the home of the Baroness. But eyes must have peeked behind lace curtains when the chauffeured limousine of Queen Juliana brought Corrie to the front door of the apartment house.

Corrie rarely spoke about her relationships with royalty. When pressed for stories about her conversations with Princess Wilhelmina (who retained that title after her abdication in favor of Queen Juliana), Corrie would become very evasive. However, from her friends in Holland, Herman and Els ter Welle, and her nephew, Bob van Woerden, we are able to catch a glimpse of her influence on world leaders.

One time, Dutch evangelist Jan van der Hoeven was holding a small Bible study for young society people who lived near the royal family. Princess Margriet was one of the participants, and frequently Corrie was asked to come and speak. When the princess married Peter van Vollenhoven, he asked, "Can we have that old lady with the naughty eyes to the wedding?"

Some time later, Peter wanted to have a Bible study about the Second Coming, and he invited a prominent university professor, a pastor, and Corrie. Corrie didn't know the views of the two men, and prayed, "Lord, I want to testify, but I do not want the professor and pastor there."

Later, Peter called her and said, "I am so sorry, Miss ten Boom, but the Bible study had to be cancelled, because the others can't come."

Corrie, containing her delight, said, "Oh, there is no reason why we can't get together anyhow."

"But just my mother-in-law [the Queen] will be there," Peter explained.

The Bible study was very small that time, but it was upon that occasion that "Peter's mother-in-law" took Corrie home.

Bob van Woerden told about a time when he received a call from the palace, where Corrie had been invited for a few days. She said, "Bob, I'm lonely. Will you come and spend some time with me?"

He met her in the garden of the Queen; as they were talking, Corrie, oblivious of appearances, reached under her dress and pulled out a handkerchief. When she was finished using it, she hiked up her dress again and returned the cloth to its hiding place.

Remembering the incident many years later, Bob, the university professor-musician, chuckled over his Tante Corrie. "She was the same everywhere she went; protocol meant very little to her."

As Ellen de Kroon followed Corrie around the world, she discovered that working as a team with this Gospel bearer could mean tea with royalty or crackers with prisoners. The stories were usually the same, and the messages just as simple for the sophisticated as they were for the uneducated.

In Lweza, Uganda, Corrie was invited to speak in a prison, and when she arrived, there were about six hundred African men dancing on the big prison square. The drums beat wildly, and the rhythm of the music caused them to move their bodies as if in a trance.

Corrie said, "Their eyes looked wild, and I felt fear creeping into my heart."

When the director ordered the men to stop dancing, they resented it and were in a sullen, angry mood when Corrie stood up. Corrie suddenly regretted that there were no other whites with her. Would her black brothers protect her? She said later, "I repented of my lack of trust, and the Lord surely spoke through me to these stranded men."

There were several stories that Corrie used for all audiences. She never assumed that everyone in an audience had made a real commitment to Jesus, no matter where she was. Like an actress in a long-running hit play, she was always fresh in her presentations. At one point, Corrie thought she would stop telling her flashlight story, but Ellen encouraged her to continue, and so she did until her speaking ability was silenced.

Another famous story was her embroidery of a crown. She would hold up the piece of cloth, first showing the beauty of the embroidered side, with all the threads forming a beautiful picture, which she described as the plan God has for our lives. Then she would flip it over to show the tangled, confused underside, illustrating how we view our lives from a human standpoint.

The rendition of this poem is uniquely Corrie's:

My life is but a weaving, between my God and me
I do not choose the colors, He worketh steadily.
Oftimes He weaveth sorrow, and I in foolish pride,
Forget He sees the upper, and I the underside.

Not till the loom is silent and the shuttles cease to fly.
Will God unroll the canvas and explain the reason why,
The dark threads are as needful in the skillful Weaver's hand,
As the threads of gold and silver in the pattern He has planned.

Ellen heard the same messages and the same stories hundreds of times, from places as remote as a Siberian village, to the dining room of the exclusive Bel Air Hotel in Beverly Hills. Yet she wrote, "I soon learned that the best thing I could do during a service was to listen in the same way that Corrie spoke—as if I were hearing the story for the first time. That way I could be an encouragement to her, and God seemed to give me new insights into her stories, too."[25]

Corrie's theology, if you could call it that, was useful, not theoretical. When people tried to get her embroiled in theological differences, she would tell about conversations she had with fellow prisoners in the concentration camp: "We were sitting around the Bible twice a day. We didn't know what church backgrounds others had, and it didn't interest us. We knew that we were facing death daily.

"I had many personal talks with my fellow prisoners. I didn't ask, 'What is your opinion about predestination?' I was not interested if the other person was a pre- or post- or amillenarian. I asked questions like: 'Do you know that Jesus died for the sins of the whole world, also for your sins, and that He loves you?'

" 'Did you give your heart to Him?' "

" 'Did you confess your sins to Him and repent?' "

"If she said, 'Yes' to such questions, and then I saw her disappear into the hospital, where most of the patients died, or if she went on her way to the gas chamber, then I was happy to know that she was safe in the arms of Jesus, who would carry her through the valley of the shadow of death to the house of the Father."

When facing death, theology is unimportant.

Before church people, Corrie was often tested about basic beliefs. Once when she was in Germany, she was talking to a men's group of Lutherans and Baptists. After her talk, she was asked, "What do you think is the biblical method of baptizing?"

In recalling this occasion, she said, "Here I saw a trick from the enemy. The blessing of that meeting could be lost if the time would be spent in arguing about baptism. I prayed for wisdom, and then answered: 'Let us read the last words Jesus spoke on earth in Mark 16:15–17 [KJV]: "Go ye into all the world, and preach the Gospel to every creature. He that believeth and is baptized shall be saved; but he that believeth not shall be damned. And these signs shall follow them that believe; in my name shall they cast out devils; they shall speak with new tongues; They shall take up serpents; and if they drink any deadly thing, it shall not hurt them; they shall lay hands on the sick, and they shall recover."

" 'What were the three important commissions that the Lord Jesus gave? First, world evangelism, second, baptism, third, gifts of the Holy Spirit.

" 'What about the first? Did you do everything to obey this joyful task of bringing the Gospel over the world by preaching, prayers, and purse?

" 'What about the third? Are people in bondage being set free by your obedience and power? Are sick people being healed in Jesus' name?

" 'If there is still something unfinished in your life as far as points one and three are concerned, then do something about it. If you are through with one and three, then come to me and I will tell you what I think about the biblical way of baptism. However, I can tell you now that the Lord has surely not meant baptism to be a means for quarreling, but to enjoy it as a great, joyful privilege.' "

While other Christians argued denominational or doctrinal differences, Corrie pointed people to Christ. She could dissolve dogmatic viewpoints in her audience by her irrepressible humor. Once she was speaking in East Berlin for a group of theologians. She told her simple stories, even for this learned group, and when it was time for questions, one of the eminent clergymen asked, "Miss ten Boom, don't you agree that women should not be allowed to teach in the church?"

Corrie was on the spot. She stood up, a radiant smile on her face, and said, *"Hallelujah, nein!"*

Brother Andrew chuckled as he told this story about his friend. "Her unique way of answering that question broke up the whole audience . . . they had no answer! From then on, her nickname in East Germany was *'Hallelujah, nein.'* "

Tact, however, was not always Corrie's strong quality. Her love for others was peppered with bluntness. One of her close friends, an outstanding English Bible teacher and evangelist, Sidney Wilson, wrote some brilliant magazine articles on biblical prophecy. Corrie wrote to him, "I enjoy your articles, but keep the tone pure and don't become a fighter, as so many have done in the United States. Whatever does it matter if others have a different opinion about the millenium? After all, the future will teach us who is right. Is it not possible to defend your opinion and still leave room for the ideas of people who think differently?"

One of the ironies of life is that Corrie was better known in Germany than she was in her native Holland. God's mysterious ways led her to the homeland of her captors, to touch so many lives. One time she was going to preach in a large cathedral in the city of Karl-Marx-Stadt. The church was so jammed that thousands couldn't get in. Corrie decided there should be loudspeakers outside, but the local authorities told her that wouldn't be possible.

Corrie said, "Take me to the highest authority in the city."

"Sir, I want loudspeakers outside the cathedral."

"Miss ten Boom, that is propaganda for religion. We can't do that in a socialist society."

Corrie pointed a finger directly at him and said, "You know Jesus is Victor, don't you?"

He looked at the finger, then at her expression, and said, "Yes, Madam."

Loudspeakers were installed, and the entire city heard her messages.

Some look at preachers, evangelists, Christian writers or teachers and wonder if their ministry is as practical as their expressions of belief. Are they genuine? Corrie has become a legend in her own time, with people around the world volunteering stories from their personal experiences. Herman ter Welle, whose life and ministry were influenced by her, said, "She was able to maintain the horizontal and vertical line of communication simultaneously. She illustrated that it was possible to do your everyday work and yet be in touch with God."

Ter Welle tells about a time when Corrie was speaking for a Full Gospel congregation in Holland. The meeting was held in a club building, which was jammed to capacity. A wooden table served as a pulpit, on a simple platform. When it was time for the service, Corrie confessed to her audience, "I was alarmed to see this open table to stand behind. Unfortunately, I have a ladder in my stocking, and everyone can see it. But now all of you know, so it need not bother me anymore."

Corrie taught her listeners, with personal and often amusing illustrations, to tell, and not hide, the things that bothered them.

Paul's words apply to her: ". . . for I have learned to be content in whatever circumstances I am. . . . I also know how to live in prosperity; in any and every circumstance I have learned the secret of being filled and going hungry, both of having abundance and suffering need" (Philippians 4:11, 12).

She had many friends in high places of business and government, men like Bill Middendorf, former United States ambassador to Holland. When Corrie spoke to the American community in the Hague, where the Middendorfs served, she also had the opportunity to speak to the Soviet ambassador to the Netherlands. She told him about loving your enemies, but he said you must hate your enemies.

Corrie, nonplussed by this reaction, smiled broadly and gave him one of her books.

Once there were two young Christian men who were imprisoned in an Eastern European country for passing out Christian literature. Corrie called Bill Middendorf at 3:00 A.M. and asked him if he could intervene for the release of these missionaries.

One of her great desires was for a revival behind the Iron Curtain, and many of her books were smuggled into Eastern Europe.

Embassies, native villages, royal courts, and prisons: The world was Corrie's mission calling. Harry Howard, the chaplain of the hard-core prison at San Quentin, told how the inmates gave her a standing ovation at the close of her morning chapel message. This had never been done for any guest at San Quentin, but they knew they were listening to an exprisoner who had done time in a place far worse than any United States penitentiary. Howard and his wife, Elva, said they had "the rare privilege of helping to fulfill the dream and vision that Corrie had of a group of volunteers going into the jails and prisons of America," as part of the Association of Christian Prison Volunteers, another organization Corrie started.

Not many have been used by God to reach millions, as Corrie has, but one story about her compassion illustrates how God uses a servant's heart.

A woman wrote to her:

> Once when I was ill in bed, you came to visit me in my little room. . . . You prayed for me, but you wanted to do something besides that to show love and kindness. It must have been a very warm day, and you thought a bath would be soothing to me. I was a little embarrassed, because I wasn't used to being undressed before anyone, but I accepted in love, because I knew God had sent you. Afterward I got to wondering why the Lord cared so much as to cause the elite of His kingdom to care about me. Never before had He sent an angel clear from Holland to bring me His love.

As Corrie and her bright, candid assistant, Ellen, began to travel around the world, it became clear that the Lord had put together these two as a team. Ellen was a nurse when Corrie needed nursing care. Corrie was the spiritual mother when Ellen was struggling with her own spiritual growth. Ellen knew how to handle Corrie, treating her with deference one moment and at other times assuming an almost motherly role.

Ellen thought that one of Corrie's most powerful illustrations of the cross of Christ was a story she told to a group of prisoners:

> Corrie tells how all of the women in the concentration camp had to stand naked in the icy cold before the eyes of the guards. It was during that time that Corrie fully understood the Cross—how terrible it was and how cruel for Jesus to have to hang before all the world in His suffering. When Jesus went to the Cross, they took His garments, He hung there naked. Through her suffering, Corrie understood a fraction of Jesus' suffering, and it made her feel so thankful. . . .
>
> How wonderful to see a tenderness and deep respect for Corrie come over the faces of those men as they began to see the story of the Cross in a new way; they felt that Corrie understood their own shame of prison life, and many were blessed that evening.[26]

As Corrie and Ellen continued to visit the palaces and prisons of the world, a new and increasingly insistent message was heard from Corrie. She talked with greater emphasis upon the end times and the Second Coming of Christ.

From the time she first began to study the Bible, Corrie learned about prophecy in relation to the end of the world as we know it. However, in the late 1960s and into the next decade, almost all of her messages included being prepared. She wrote:

> We believe that in our day we can see clearly the outlines of Biblical prophecies in world history. It is good to compare the newspapers with the Bible at this time. Then we understand that Jesus may come very soon. Before His return there will be a hard battle, and therefore it is good to prepare ourselves and to gird our loins with power.[27]

As she marched into the 1970s, this warning message became stronger. While most women her age are struggling between despair and indifference to surrounding conditions, Corrie was saying, "We have to proclaim loudly that the end is near, so that people will be startled out of their everyday rest and security by this godly message."

The friend of ambassadors and beggars was soon given the chance to proclaim her words of encouragement and warning with a certain trumpet. Into the spotlight of media fame stepped our surprised performer, an octogenarian on center stage.

19

A Star Is Born Again

In 1970 Corrie was in Holland, weak and sick, convinced that her traveling days were numbered. She had been ordered to rest for at least five months, and the burden of her speaking commitments weighed heavily upon her.

However, if ever a person doubts the power of intercessory prayer, he only needs to follow the saga of Corrie. At a time when she was curtailing her activities, a group of women who had planned to have her speak for their retreat in Arrowhead Springs, California, were praying that the Lord would restore her health. One woman wrote her, "The Lord just spoke to me and assured me that all will be well concerning you and the retreat."

No mere human doctor could equal the healing power of the Great Physician. Ellen packed their red suitcases, and off they went on another adventure. For the first time, however, she pushed Corrie in wheelchairs, through the airports. From then on, the wheelchairs of the world became rolling gospel chariots. Every airport attendant and Red Cap who found himself pushing Corrie also had a mini-sermon on what it means to be born again.

Corrie did not strive for fame, but her prolific pen resulted in books that were read by thousands throughout the world. However, it wasn't until the 1970s that her story spread in wider circles. One of her books was *A Prisoner and Yet,* the poignant story of her life in Ravensbruck. The talented writing team of John and Tibby Sherrill read her memoirs. While working on a book, *God's Smuggler,* with Brother Andrew, they heard more about this remarkable Dutch woman and were convinced they should write her story.

The Sherrills and Corrie clicked, and from this working, praying team came one of the outstanding best-sellers of the era, *The Hiding Place.* This book, written in first person, but reading like an adventure novel, was Corrie's springboard to fame.

Publishing wheels were spinning with the hottest commodity in the Christian book field. Another prominent writer, Jamie Buckingham, met Corrie at a writer's conference, and the groundwork was laid for a second record-breaking best-seller. When Buckingham met Corrie, his first impression was that she was stubborn. He recalled, "She looked me over, said a sort of 'Hrrumph!' in a Dutch accent, and began to talk about the Lord. We hit it off at once."

Buckingham was invited to have dinner with Corrie, and she served smoked eel and raw herring, asking him to take his choice. Wanting to make a good impression, and also be polite, he chose the eel, since it was slippery and he thought it would slide down quickly and be gone. His mistake was, it slid back up just as rapidly as it slid down, and he had to rush to the bathroom.

When he returned, thoroughly humiliated, Corrie was doubled over with laughter. "We'll work well together," she said. "Any man who is not ashamed to throw up will tell an honest story."

As Buckingham and Corrie made plans to work on *Tramp for the Lord,* he learned Corrie had discussed this book with three different publishers. Though no publishing contracts had been signed, each of the three firms was under the impression it was to publish this book of Corrie's. Corrie was less concerned about the publishing arrangements than she was about getting as many books as possible out there to the readers! Buckingham, amused, but appalled at the prospect of them working with three publishers on the same book, said, "I convinced her that though we were writing for the glory of God—to reach scores of thousands of souls—we could only contract with one firm to publish *Tramp for the Lord.* She asked me if I could fix the mess." In spite of the publishing complications, *Tramp for the Lord* and *The Hiding Place* both went on to become worldwide best-sellers.

In the secular field, best-selling books, if they have dramatic and public appeal, may be scouted as movie possibilities. In the Christian market, this is not a usual procedure. However, Ruth Graham was one of the first persons to see the film potentials in *The Hiding Place.* She and Billy were friends of Corrie, having met in 1960, and they had been impressed by the woman who had suffered so much, yet had such a twinkle in her eyes. Ruth and Billy had dubbed her one of "God's merry saints."

As the possibility of having a movie made of her life became closer to being reality, Corrie saw it as another link in Betsie's vision to tell the world about God's love and forgiveness. If the prospect of such fame seemed awesome to her, Corrie didn't show it. In 1972, shortly after the publication of *The Hiding Place,* Corrie wrote Marian Johnson, her original American benefactor:

> Next week we go to Glendale to meet the people of World Wide Pictures. Billy Graham is very happy with the book and that it can be worked out in a movy [yes, that's the way she spelled it].
>
> It surely will reach many more people than we have ever been able to reach. I am so thankfull. John Sherrill's book, *The Hiding Place,* is a good seller and has opened many doors and hearts for me. In April I'll be 80 years, and it seems that the Lord gives me more and more joyful work to do. I feel so privileged.
>
> God uses Ellen much. Her testimonies are so powerfull and always bring a blessing. We both feel happy to be in the U.S.A.

As the conferences and planning began for the film undertaking, it was predominant in the minds of all the participants that *The Hiding Place* was going to be a different type of Christian film. World Wide Pictures, the motion picture arm of the Billy Graham Association, with its creative professionalism, became a major force in the industry.

The combined talents of many people, working and praying together, were to produce a movie that changed the public's concept of Christian movie making. Corrie had frequently visited Edgar and Thelma Elfstrom before moving to southern California. Edgar, a prominent newspaper publisher who served on the board of Corrie's management group, strongly supported Corrie's new film endeavor and helped make *The Hiding Place* a reality.

Bill Brown, executive producer of the film, and others working with him encountered challenges that were beyond any they had experienced in producing previous church films. At one low point in the progress of the film, it seemed that plans would have to be cancelled. The budget was only $1.5 million, which is small in comparison to most multi-million-dollar Hollywood productions, but they didn't have enough money to get started. Then another miracle in the life of Corrie occurred. Some good friends called her and volunteered to give a large sum of money toward the film.

When Corrie was in need, she usually said, "Our heavenly Father owns the cattle on a thousand hills. We'll have to ask Him to sell a cow."

Her reaction to the news of the financial windfall was, "Praise the Lord! He sold a cow!"

With the project out of the planning stage, Bill Brown suggested a plan for a Hiding Place Family. With over 40,000 of Corrie's friends and fans around the world, there soon developed an unprecedented list of people who promised to pray and pledged to give toward the film on a regular basis.

As people prayed, God prepared talented individuals to undertake the film. A key person in movie making is the director, but when a very skilled director, Jimmy Collier, was asked to take the position, he blurted out, "I can't do it."

Why would he turn down such an enticing assignment? Collier recalled his vivid impressions of the Holocaust, when he was a boy in high school. "I was drawn to it and repelled by it at the same time. I identified so much with these people being separated from their families, and this darkness would come over me. I couldn't handle it."

Collier was such a natural for the job. He had done a film in Israel, called *His Land,* and he loved and identified with the Jews. However, he knew that the world didn't really care about the Holocaust, and the thought of making a film about that era almost made him ill.

He prayed for a long time that the Lord would show him if he was the man for making this film. One day he read a Scripture that directed his decision: "This is my work, and I can do it only because Christ's mighty energy is at work within me" (Colossians 1:29 TLB).

The subsequent relationship between Jimmy Collier, the eloquent and skilled director, and Corrie, the woman who became a film star in her eighties, resulted in five films. Their teamwork began with *The Hiding Place* as Collier reached into Corrie's thoughts and emotions, determined to unearth more than the surface stories that were in the book.

For years Corrie had told her story over and over again. To transfer her character and the characters of her family members into the flesh and blood of actors and actresses, would take more than lines to say. Collier became the catalyst between Corrie and the reality of the players who portrayed her family.

He said, "I was able to pull things out of her, but they were there to pull. Many painful stories came out about the prison days. I believe there was a hedge around Corrie and Betsie, and I don't think they saw many things in that awful barracks."

From Collier to the actors and actresses who made the film come alive, God was guiding the choice of the right people. The demanding role of Corrie went to Jeannette Clift, a talented Broadway actress with no experience in films. Julie Harris, longtime Hollywood star, accepted the role of Betsie. Arthur O'Connell, a man with fifty screen roles to his credit, portrayed Father ten Boom so well that Corrie had tears in her eyes the first time she saw him in the part. Eileen Heckart, Oscar winner, played Katje, a concentration-camp prisoner. This was an impressive cast for a small-studio production!

For five months the actors and crew worked in Holland and England, filming the powerful story. While they worked, Corrie and thousands of her prayer partners prayed. The Hiding Place Family was a unique group in the history of movie making.

Collier told about one amusing sidelight of the production. When the location for the Beje set was chosen, it was built in the red-light district of Haarlem. While the filming was going on, the flow of traffic was slowed through the area, and the prostitutes were very angry about losing business. One day these women trooped into the production office and demanded to be paid, because their business was suffering.

How would you react while watching the story of your life unfold in living color? Corrie could not be a detached observer; she was candid about her emotions. After observing the action on location, she wrote: "It was rather strange to walk into the watch shop and discover German soldiers there. Something went all through me, but I experienced again how deep and great is God's forgiveness. The actor portraying Papa (who is very much like my papa) and the actresses playing the parts of Betsie and me all entered the street.

What a special moment that was, to see a whole new family of mine!"

During the filming, Ellen sent out prayer letters to friends. One of the strongest requests was "that each person in the crew will be touched by the Holy Spirit and that the Christians will show that Jesus Christ is the Truth, the Life, and the Way to the non-Christians, even when difficulties arise and the devil is testing their weaknesses."

Sometimes Corrie's presence on the set was unnerving. On the last day of filming, Frank Jacobson, the producer, had brought her in to watch a scene. Jeannette, as Corrie, was to walk through the gate of Ravensbruck, limping to freedom, bewildered by her unexpected release from the death camp. It disturbed Jeannette, having Corrie watching her, and the scene didn't seem to come together. Collier, recalling that day, said, "After all, you just couldn't go over to Corrie and say, 'Will you please leave?' It was her life."

Finally, Jeannette, consummate actress that she is, finished the scene as the real Corrie watched and nodded her approval.

In the summer of 1975 the film was done, and the haunting music of Tedd Smith, Billy Graham's crusade pianist, was woven into the motion picture. Corrie and Ellen were in Haarlem, working with me on a third major book, *In My Father's House,* when arrangements were made for a preview in a theater on the Grote Markt, where over thirty years before the German occupying forces sought to destroy and demoralize the townspeople. Special invitations had been issued to friends in Haarlem and the surrounding towns, and the moment was tense when the film began. Many sitting in the audience had been extras in the film; others remembered World War II vividly. Partway through the showing, during the scene in Haarlem when the ten Booms were arrested, one woman in the audience let out a cry and ran out the back door. Later, during the harsh concentration-camp scenes, others left. Corrie was oblivious to these exits, concentrating only upon the unfolding of the story.

Corrie and Ellen felt it was ironic that *The Hiding Place,* dedicated to proclaiming the love of Christ no matter how desperate the circumstances, would be previewed in a run-down little movie house which customarily showed X-rated films.

The world premiere was scheduled for September 29, 1975, in the heart of glamor city, Beverly Hills, California. Billy Graham, Roy and Dale Rogers, Pat Boone, the stars of the film, and hundreds of prominent people were invited. But the real star was everybody's grandmother, the lively lady in the bright formal: Corrie herself.

The audience had just begun to quiet down when there was a loud crack, like a rifle shot, and after a slight commotion, everyone was told to leave the theater. The audience filed out calmly, and soon the hall was filled with tear gas. It was later discovered that a member of the American Nazi party had tossed the bomb, evidently as a gesture of hatred for the message of love for the Jews in *The Hiding Place.*

As Corrie would say, in piercing simplicity, "The devil is strong, but Jesus is stronger." From near disaster, the bomb episode turned into triumph. Cliff Barrows, Billy Graham, Pat Boone, Corrie, and others led gospel singing outside, and an old-fashioned street meeting was held in the midst of sophisticated Beverly Hills. The publicity, which couldn't have been bought for thousands of dollars, went around the world.

However, at first Corrie was dejected. All the work, the planning, and the elaborate arrangements seemed to have been wasted. Her doctor from Holland, Dr. Hans Moolenburgh, immediately came to her side, concerned that the strain of the evening would be too much for her. Corrie listened to the speeches from the notables on the platform in front of the theater and, turning to Dr. Moolenburgh, with a lilt in her voice, said, "Did you hear what Billy Graham said? . . . that I am one of God's greatest saints." Dr. Moolenburgh, standing with her nephew, Peter van Woerden, said, "Don't talk nonsense, Tante Corrie, Peter and I both know that's not true."

As the film began playing around the country, the reviews ranged from cynical to glowing. One reviewer called it "a very hard sell." The criticism was, "Corrie ten Boom is obviously a wonderful human being, but she is also a saleslady for the Bible and the Billy Graham interpretation of that which is found therein."

Another, more sympathetic review glowed with praise: "I don't know whether the finished product—scheduled to be released at key premieres in selected cities throughout the United States, will win any Academy Awards or not. But if awards are made for integrity, sensitivity, humanity and spirit, this film will sweep them all."

Corrie became the darling of the American evangelicals and the most sought after woman speaker in the world. Wherever she went, people recognized her. Some wanted to hug her, and that's when her guard would go up. "Please, Ellen, keep the neck-huggers away!"

Corrie was not a woman amassing a fortune; she was the head of many ministries, channeling what she earned to needy Christian causes around the world. Her finances, contracts, speaking engagements, and personal affairs were managed by Christians, Incorporated. Walter Gastil, a retired insurance executive, was the first to head her management team. One comment in the minutes of a 1974 board meeting exemplifies the worldwide impact of one woman. It said, succinctly, "Corrie is becoming a gigantic undertaking."

Age didn't matter, health was unimportant, Corrie would continue and no one could deny that her power came from a higher source. Once she was invited to speak in Jerusalem, at a conference of four or five thousand people. She was the star of the conference and talked for over an hour. Finally, she said, "Well, I stop now, otherwise the people get too tired."

As the adulation grew, Corrie sometimes could be very curt with her admirers. She especially disliked the picture takers who would suddenly come up to her and say, "Smile, Aunt Corrie." She turned to one amateur photographer and said, "I'm talking about the Lord, not me."

While in Israel, she presented copy number 2 million of *The Hiding Place* to Golda Meir and then went with her into a private room at the Knesset, to pray with her for peace.

Another woman preacher, Kathryn Kuhlman, was in Jerusalem at the same time, and one night she called for Corrie. She was disturbed about her gift of healing and told Corrie she couldn't understand why the Holy Spirit was curing an old man, when a beautiful little girl was dying. How revealing it is to discover that the same questions plague Christian leaders that bother new believers. Corrie talked to Kathryn Kuhlman far into the night, in spite of the fact that her own health was precarious.

Also in Israel, Corrie suffered a slight heart attack, but within two days was on her feet and back at her schedule. When they left the country, a solicitous flight attendant patted her condescendingly on the shoulder and said, "Now, lady, don't be afraid. I've flown over thirty-four countries in the last ten years, and nothing ever happened."

Corrie was being pushed in her wheelchair by Dr. Moolenburgh, who accompanied her to the Jerusalem conference. She looked at the attendant and said in a tone unlike that one would expect of the weak individual she appeared to be, "Sir, I have ministered in over sixty-four countries, and nothing ever happened to me . . . so don't you be afraid."

The steward looked down at her wrinkled face, her coil of gray hair, and said to Dr. Moolenburgh, "A minister in sixty-four countries! Is that really true?"

Corrie's life was bigger than imagination!

Hundreds of requests for speaking engagements continued to pour into Christians, Incorporated. Dozens of babies were named Corrie, and even a bulldog was named after her. She was called "one of the towering women of our time," and "one of the most beautiful people of our time," and received more accolades than most human beings could handle. She turned down an invitation to be grand marshal of the Pasadena Rose Parade, with a mere shrug of her shoulders and her frequent expression, "I don't think that's important." She was a woman who did not let circumstances overwhelm her. She wore the world like a loose garment that she could step out of at will.

As she began to appear on television, speak at the Billy Graham crusades, and become a household word in evangelical circles, there was an acceleration of urgency in her messages about the Second Coming of Christ. She wrote in her magazine, *The Hiding Place,* these words:

> As we go into 1977, the coming of the Lord Jesus is a lot nearer than when we first believed. We can expect Him soon. Let's keep looking for Him and expecting His coming. Two Bible books from which I gain practical help are the letters from Paul to Timothy. Twice in those letters Paul talks about "fighting the good fight of faith." He does not say, 'See that you fight well,' but 'fight the good fight.' "

The old warrior was fighting a good fight.

20

The Halo Tightens

Fame can be as demanding as it is fleeting. Many who achieve it feel that they have finally received their just reward for their work of sacrifice. "I deserved it," is the attitude. To Corrie, fame was a result in God's plan, not the culmination of personal triumph. She wore it with amusement and sometimes irritation.

But she became a heroine at a time when the American public was hungry for heroes. One of her Dutch friends said, "Americans spoil a preacher." Corrie knew this and enjoyed it. Many times she would return to Holland and say, "It is so hard to preach here." She did not have the audience or the adulation that she received in the United States. Part of the reason, perhaps, was because her World War II experiences were shared by many who never achieved the degree of importance she did. However, her home-country critics neglected to understand the ministry of forgiveness and the selfless, homeless tramping she did for so many decades, to spread this message around the world.

As hundreds of requests for speaking engagements poured in to Christians, Incorporated, her board of directors realized that to conserve her strength they needed to arrange for fewer, larger meetings. Billy Graham had her appear at his crusades; television programs vied to interview her; thousands would crowd into stadiums to hear her, with more waiting outside.

By this time, her companion, Ellen, had become an accomplished travel arranger, letter writer, and speaker. Then at the height of Corrie's activities and popularity, Ellen fell in love. She had never felt that God had called her to be single, as He had Corrie. However, as the years went by and she was still tramping around the world in Corrie's shadow, she began to doubt that any man would want her. She waited and prayed, and when Corrie was speaking at Oral Roberts University, Ellen met the chaplain, Bob Stamps, who was destined to be her husband. But how could she tell Corrie?

Corrie may have been old, but she wasn't stupid. She discerned the signs of love between Ellen and Bob before they did and began to pray for a new companion.

One Sunday afternoon in 1976, a beautiful, soft-spoken English girl, Pam Rosewell, was also praying for God's will in her life. She had just read Ephesians 2:10: "For we are His workmanship, created in Christ Jesus for good works, which God prepared beforehand, that we should walk in them," when Ellen called her and said that Tante Corrie would like to see her. Pam had worked for Brother Andrew for more than seven years and was no stranger to Corrie.

Pam knew that the "good works" God had prepared for her were to be used as Corrie's new teammate. And what a whirlwind it turned out to be! From meetings with publishers to universities to receive honorary degrees, from Canadian television programs to a conference at a Christian center in California, all in the first few weeks, was a challenge to Pam's organizational ability. She learned to steer Corrie through crowds for rapid getaways, to have water available at the speaker's dais, to make sure there were no flash photos taken after the first few minutes of speaking, in addition to being personal helper, travel agent, and confidante. Pam was crisp, British, and efficient for the rigors of the celebrity circuit. She tried to shield Corrie from too many demands.

However, Corrie could not be shielded from herself. She was a worker; a visionary; a leader with high expectations. When you were with Corrie, you gave her your full attention, not because she wanted personal flattery, but because she had a sense of urgency for her ministry; the peripheral issues of this earthly life faded in importance.

In her eighty-fifth year, the Lord gave her a new plan for her life. She moved into a beautiful home in California, where she had a bed of her own, a place to sit and dictate her books, a dining room to entertain friends, an organ, and a garden, profuse with flowers and birds.

She wrote to Marian Johnson, her friend for so many years:

> I always had the grace to be a tramp, and whenever I felt sorry for myself I would say, "Lord Jesus, You suffered so much for me. If I have to suffer just a little bit for You, I will." And I was happy in the work the Lord had given me. But now that I am no longer a tramp, I am so happy to have my own home and believe it will be very fruitful in the Lord's service. Pray for the books that will be born here.

Corrie loved America and realized that the mass media gave her so many opportunities for the messages that God put on her heart that establishing a permanent home in her adopted country was His will. In January, 1977, the United States consul in Holland gave Pam and Corrie resident-alien status, so they could remain as long as they wished.

In Holland, the Beje, which had attracted thousands of visitors from around the world, was finally closed to tourist traffic, and Corrie's ties to her homeland seemed permanently severed.

Corrie was so happy with her California home. Friends gave her house-warming showers, and ladies in local churches provided her with everything from pans to plants. One friend, Betsy Chapple, helped with the decorating and tried to put together the house in a Dutch fashion. "I found it difficult to watch Corrie, who had always been a giver, be able to accept things gracefully. At first she didn't want to take things, but everyone was so anxious to do for her."

Was Shalom House a retirement home? Corrie didn't know the meaning of the word. She said, "The Lord has told me I will write five books and do five movies here." No one disputed her when she said, "The Lord has told me." But the skeptics began to count on their fingers. She was right about the five films, but wrong about the books. She wrote six before her first stroke.

As she began her time of disciplined work, aided by her competent secretary-companion, Corrie astounded everyone. She gave hope to those who fear growing old, continuing to set goals and meeting challenges. In her book *A Tramp Finds a Home* she wrote:

The Lord Jesus has the first place in this house. He has given us much important work to do here, and it is because we are doing His will that He blesses the home. Apart from the writing of books and the making of films, there is intercession from this house, plus counseling personally and by telephone and letter. Through reading books and magazines that inform us of current events, we keep ourselves up-to-date with local, national and international affairs.[28]

One way she sought to improve herself was by watching videotapes of her talks. She would critique her delivery and methods and ask others to do the same. Jimmy Collier described her as "made for the media," and Jeannette Clift called her "the finest actress I have known."

Life is not without its common challenges, and plumbing is one of them. One night the water heater in the house burst, and Corrie went to a neighbor to report that water was ankle deep in the kitchen and she didn't know what to do. The fire department arrived with blaring sirens, and as the firemen brought in their pumps, a crowd gathered on the sidewalk. Corrie stood watching the four firemen work, knowing that she had a captive audience and only a short time to talk. She said, "Do you men know Jesus Christ? He is a friend of mine, and I'd like to introduce Him to you."

The firemen kept on working, no doubt thinking, *What kind of nut is this old lady? Let's hurry and get out of here.*

Corrie gave them four copies of *The Hiding Place* and walked out to the street, thanking them for coming to help when they were so needed. But the sight that greeted her was not what she expected. Her neighbors, some of whom she hadn't met before, were watching the commotion. After she explained what had happened inside, she said, "I am Corrie ten Boom, and I've been wanting to know my neighbors. Do you know my friend, Jesus Christ? I would like to introduce Him to you sometime. How about coming over to see me next Tuesday evening at 7:30, and we'll get acquainted."

From a broken water heater came new souls into God's kingdom and the nucleus of people for her first Bible-study group.

Corrie the legend was a miracle of this century, a woman of such surrender to the Lord Jesus that her total dedication was to do His work. If she had been an actress in the secular world, she probably would have won Academy Awards. If she had been a novelist or social critic her writings might have taken a Nobel Prize. But God chose to use her because she was an available tool.

However, it is dangerous to deify a human, and Corrie's feet had clay, although not as mired as most of us. A pastor in Virginia, James Parker, wrote, "Corrie is one of the Lord's most special servants in this century, and yet for those who know her well she is a real character at times, and not at all the sweet little old lady a lot of Christians have thought her to be."

Corrie wanted center stage when she was talking about her messages, her work. When the subject matter would change or interest wane, she might say she was tired and take a nap. She could be very impatient if she thought you were not concentrating on her. When I was working with her on *In My Father's House,* she would stop while I was groping for words and pray. "Father, help Carole straighten out her thinking and give her wisdom for her questions." Without pausing for a breath she would say, "Now what is it you wanted to ask?"

One friend of hers said, "Please don't write any more 'Corriology.' We've had enough of that." Whether or not that was a valid concern, it is impossible to minimize the impact this woman has made upon lives. Many people have written saying that they were "Corrie's very best friends" or, "We knew her better than anyone." She did have many female friends; but she was predominantly male oriented. The men in her life were those strong individuals, successful in their own professions or ministries, who supported, but did not idolize Corrie. Bill Butler, with his wife, Bettie, headed her organization Christians, Inc. Surely he saw her in relation to the one area where people show their true character: in dealing with money. Bill said, "Corrie had fewer faults than anyone I've known. She refused to listen to, watch, or participate in garbage, and Scripture was hidden inside her. Money made no difference to her . . . she would have given it all away."

The Corrie ten Boom ministries expanded, with many missionaries and projects supported by her earnings throughout the world. She became more than an evangelist-writer: She became an institution!

The Butlers said, "Few Christians take risks. Corrie would take risks, and when the big time came, it was just one more challenge for her to meet. God created a strong leader for our time—someone who went through things we fear, to show us that He will take care of us."

One of her dominant themes, especially in her later years, was prophetic in nature. Corrie said that Anna, who was a prophetess in the Bible, was a woman she could relate to. Herbert Lockyer, in his *All the Women of the Bible,* says, "To prophesy simply means to proclaim a divine message, and Anna was one to whom it was given to know events before and after, and one through whom God spoke to others."[29]

James Parker said: "Corrie's message to the Body of Christ is 'no pit is so deep that God's love is not deeper still' and 'in every situation, no matter what the circumstances, Jesus is Victor!' This is a wonderful message, because it is a message of hope based on the eternal faithfulness and love of God, rather than our changing circumstances. We believe Corrie because she has been to the hell of Hitler's concentration camp and come back to tell us that even in the darkest of circumstances, the Lord was with her, and Jesus was very much the Victor. That is especially encouraging to those of us who live in these turbulent times.

"I believe that Corrie's ministry will live far beyond her life on this earth and will continue to touch millions of lives with hope and encouragement and conviction until Jesus comes again.

"Corrie told me once that she felt her ministry of thirty-three years had been to prepare the church to suffer. Her ministry, then, has not only been one of hope and encouragement, but one of prophetic preparation for the hours ahead for the church."

God brought team workers in Corrie's life, who were able to implement her visions in a practical way. Jimmy Collier was one of those persons. When she called him and said, "The Lord has told me we're going to make five films," Collier wasn't sure what that prophecy meant, but he did know Corrie's determination. One thing she wanted to do was to make a film for prisoners.

Jimmy looked at Corrie, then thought of the demography of modern prison society. Here she was, in her eighties, wanting to communicate to young, mostly black prisoners. "I had all my doubts, so I cooked up questions to put her on the defensive. I sat there in her backyard and slammed her with questions.

"Corrie, we're going to play a game—and I'm going to say things that all of these people in the front row will say."

Her eyes twinkled because she loved games and improvisations. It was like charades with her.

"Look, lady, I'm just a number, a prisoner in a computer society. When you're through talkin' God stuff, you're just going to walk out of here, and I go back behind the bars."

Corrie answered the imaginary prisoner, talking about being a number. As Collier bombarded her, she talked back, and out of this the script was written for the prison film.

Collier said, "Corrie is an actress in the best sense of the word. When we were shooting the prison film, Pam would bring her to the studio, and she would go to the bathroom and throw up. She'd say, 'I can't remember any more.' There's a terrible pressure when you're old, and Corrie would get terrible headaches.

"Pam would come in and say, 'She's very ill today and vomiting.' Then a half hour later she would show up on the set, and we'd go on."

Corrie, who grew up in a home disapproving of movies, became a consummate actress after the first biographical film. She learned, also, from Jeannette Clift. Although their relationship on the set was very loving, they became very close after the film was finished, when they shared the platform as conference speakers. Jeannette learned one of the great secrets in relating to her; they enjoyed jokes and good humor. She found, however, it was difficult to be in Corrie's shadow. People would say, "I just want to touch you, because I can't touch Corrie."

However, when Corrie touched lives, it could leave lasting results. Jeannette said, "I have turned down scripts because I did not want anything to be an offense to Corrie."

For most of us, spiritual giants are so far out of our reach that we are intimidated. Corrie could be commanding, opinionated, and yet so simple that you were disarmed. A Dallas businesswoman, Mary Crowley, told how she had provided Corrie with an apartment when she was speaking in that area; the modern gadgets in the kitchenette were so intriguing to her famous guest that she played with them, like a child. Corrie also loved Mrs. Crowley's little white dog and would say, "Samantha must have been born before the Fall, for she certainly doesn't have any faults."

What a contrasting personality! Demanding, yet dependent. Brilliantly perceptive, yet curiously childlike.

As Corrie worked on her books, entertained, counseled with visitors, and planned more films, she told Pam of a recurring dream. In the morning she would awaken and say, "Pam, I had that dream again."

She would see herself in a room where she couldn't get out. It was almost like a prison. But while she was in this room, she saw her messages going out on television.

As she looked around her beautiful home, outside to the profuse California flowers and the well-tended garden, the prospect of being imprisoned seemed improbable.

The day came when Corrie forgot her dream and was certain the Lord was going to take her home. Her heart was going more and more slowly, sometimes down to twenty beats a minute. She wrote, "The best is yet to be. Now I might go Home, to see Jesus face to face. From service good to service best. What joyful work there would be for me in heaven!"

But her medical advisors told her that she could live longer by having a pacemaker. Corrie wasn't sure that this artificial means of staying alive was right for a child of God, so she prayed and asked for prayers from her friends. When she was certain the Lord had more work for her to do, she consented to the operation. She claimed this verse:

> For to me to live is Christ, and to die is gain. If it is to be life in the flesh, that means fruitful labor for me. Yet which I shall choose I cannot tell. I am hard pressed between the two. My desire is to depart and be with Christ, for that is far better. But to remain in the flesh is more necessary on your account. Convinced of this, I know that I shall remain and continue with you all, for your progress and joy in the faith.
>
> Philippians 1:21–25 RSV

Before she went into the operating room, Corrie lay on a gurney in the hall. Since she thought she might not have much more time on earth, she called over two orderlies and asked them if they knew her Lord Jesus Christ and then proceeded with one of her mini-sermons.

A friend asked her, during her recovery from the operation, how she handled the pain. She said she reached up and saw the hand of Jesus, with nail holes in it. Then she knew that He bore the pain upon the cross, and her pain left her.

As the pacemaker ticked off more time for the Lord's work, Corrie continued to write. She completed a beautiful book of daily devotions, *Each New Day.* In 1978, when the Christian Booksellers Convention was to be held in Denver, secret plans were underway by her publisher and World Wide Pictures to film a program before two thousand people, called *Corrie: The Lives She's Touched.* The invitations went out to people all over the world, and the plans were underway for a tribute that would be historic.

The question was, would Corrie be able to live to participate in this great occasion? Her doctor recommended that she should try some higher elevation before undertaking the trip. One day Betsy Chapple loaded Corrie, Pam, and an oxygen tank into the car and drove to the nearby San Bernardino mountains. After a short walk, Corrie wanted some cookies, so they could have a proper English tea when they returned to the cabin. She sat down under a tree, enjoying the birds and the squirrels, when she saw the children coming home from school. She called, "Hey, would you like a cookie?" Slowly, the children began to gather, as they always did around this twinkly old lady, and she told them Bible stories. After all, time was valuable.

With the question of altitude settled, Corrie went to Denver, shielded by Pam from knowing that people were coming from all over the world for the major production. When the big night came, Corrie was ready. Her close friend Cliff Barrows was the master of ceremonies, and as one accolade after another was given to her, Corrie became more radiant. Cliff Barrows said, "There are thousands of Christians who have been motivated and encouraged in their Christian walk and witness, through your example—countless lives that you have touched.

"But, Tante Corrie, I remember what you told me three or four years ago. You were sitting in our home, talking, one night, and you said, 'You know I come to America, and the halo gets so heavy on my head.' "

But Corrie's way of handling adulation was to take each compliment as a flower and then gather them all into a bouquet and give them back to Jesus by saying, "Here, Lord, they belong to You!"

When the Denver program was over, Corrie was presented with a beautiful bouquet of flowers, and skilled performer that she was, she looked up to heaven, her face a portrait of love, and raised her bouquet to the Lord.

Somewhere between beautiful humility and an almost unbelievable strength and indomitable spirit was the real Corrie. Not just a "sweet little grandmother," but a two-fisted old Dutch soldier for Jesus.

But the prison dream persisted. Soon after the "center stage" triumph in Denver, that dream came true. She became a prisoner again.

One of the poems she loved exemplifies the next chapter in her incredible book of life:

> Make me a captive, Lord,
> And then I shall be free;
> Force me to render up my sword,
> And I shall conqueror be.
> I sink in life's alarms
> When by myself I stand;
> Imprison me within Thine arms,
> And strong shall be my hand.
>
> GEORGE MATHESON

21

The Still Voice

"And we know that God causes all things to work together for good to those who love God, to those who are called according to His purpose" (Romans 8:28).

Corrie's dream of being in a "sort of prison" became a reality in August of 1978, when Pam found her in bed, unable to move or speak, the victim of a severe stroke. While she was in intensive care, her close friends were sure that she was going to heaven. Many thought, *God has used her as one of the great communicators of our time. Why would He incapacitate her so that this great gift would be silenced?*

Human rationale and God's will are not always compatible. Who can determine the unfathomable motives of our Creator?

After three weeks in the hospital, Corrie begged to go home (communicating without speech), and a new phase in her life began. She received physical and speech therapy and gradually improved. Although she couldn't speak full sentences or write, she could communicate through single words and a variety of hand signals.

Did she ever doubt the Lord during the months of struggle that followed? A Christian witness meets its true test in times of suffering. Pastor, Chuck Mylander, visited her often after her first crippling stroke, and only once did he see her upset about her own needs. As is very common in stroke patients a wave of doubt about the Lord's nearness had swept over her. Pam Rosewell explained what Corrie couldn't fully communicate, and as he questioned Corrie, tears coursed across her wrinkled cheeks.

Pastor Mylander took out his Bible and read from Matthew 28, where Jesus said, "Lo, I am with you always, even to the end of the age." He reminded Corrie that this promise was for those who gave themselves to fulfill the Great Commission, as she had done so faithfully. Her face brightened as she began to speak with confidence, "Always, always, always." Mylander, remembering that tender moment, said, "The joy of the Lord returned. Only later did I learn that this passage was one of Tante Corrie's favorites."

Pam's role was suddenly switched, by circumstance, from that of an assistant to that of a nurse. She remembered that Corrie had often said, "Pam, it is not so much what happens, but how we take it that is important. This is part of the training for the end battle."

As Corrie became a little stronger, a few people were allowed to visit her. Everyone who came to Shalom House testified about the beauty and pervasive peace that permeated Corrie's room. At one point several pastors and members of her board anointed her and prayed for her healing. Pastor Mylander recalled, "Although some people seemed to claim her healing that day, the Lord did not give me any special faith to believe that she would again be whole, healthy, and return to full vitality of public speaking and writing. However, I did believe that God would work out His purposes through her suffering, and indeed He is. I have watched it unfolding before my eyes, in quiet ways, but in ways that will count for eternity."

Seven months after her first stroke, Corrie wanted to see her friend and doctor from Holland. Hans Moolenburgh had been told by a friend, "Poor Tante Corrie, she's nothing any more. A child of five." However, when he entered her house, she was standing, waiting for him. A man with a rollicking sense of humor, who could tease Corrie in any situation, he said that he looked into her beautiful, slightly mocking, blue eyes and said, "Why, Aunt Corrie, I expected to find a senile old lady, but you are all there!"

Hans Moolenburgh, Pam, Corrie, and I prayed, as was Corrie's custom, at the end of our visit together. Although Corrie's words were unintelligible, occasionally we could discern an English word or a Dutch phrase, and there was such loving communication with the Lord she served, that I shall never forget that prayer time. The only clear words she could say were those that were characteristic of her finality in prayer, "Hallelujah, amen."

I thought of the verse "And in the same way the Spirit also helps our weakness; for we do not know how to pray as we should, but the Spirit Himself intercedes for us with groanings too deep for words" (Romans 8:26).

Corrie's greatest ministry began when God removed her verbal and writing communication skills. She was able to show all who knew her in the last years of her life that He is "always, always, always," with us.

Lotte Reimeringer, a longtime friend from Holland, who had been with Corrie when she founded the rehabilitation home after World War II, came from Holland to help take care of her. During the daytime hours, one or the other was constantly with her, sitting quietly, reading, or singing. Pam said, "All her life Tante Corrie has pointed people to the Lord Jesus Christ and urged them to trust Him. She is still doing it. Lotte and I are amazed at Corrie's perseverance in communication; although very limited in her ability to express herself, she will try and not give up. We sometimes wonder how it is possible and then remember a story that Tante Corrie told so often. As a child she said to her father, 'Daddy, I don't think I could suffer or be a martyr for Jesus Christ. My faith is not strong enough.' Her father said, 'Corrie, when you go by train from Haarlem to Amsterdam, when do I give you the train ticket? Several days before?'

" 'No, Daddy, the day I go to travel.'

" 'And so it is with God. Now you do not need the grace to suffer, but if the moment comes when you need it, He will give you the grace. He will give you the train ticket right on time.' "

Pam continued, "The Lord is giving Tante Corrie her 'train ticket.' . . . His grace for this time of need. I had always seen the Lord Jesus in her, but now in her present physical weakness, I see Him so much more clearly. She is always pointing Lotte and me to Him—sometimes literally with her hand as she points to heaven and says with a radiant face, 'I cannot . . . but He . . . He can.' "

As people came into her home, their lives were changed by her attitude. She didn't need to speak. One woman, Martha Pope, who worked in the house, said, "Corrie is such a blessing to be around and witness her faith, patience, love for Jesus, and her gratitude."

Her night nurse, Ruth Jean, said that the first week she worked for her she saw three angels at the foot of her bed. In our scientific society, the presence of angels may sound like hallucinations, but we cannot deny that the Bible says, "For He will give His angels charge concerning you, to guard you in all your ways" (Psalms 91:11).

Other times in Corrie's life when she felt the presence of angels were: taking her Bible past the guard at Ravensbruck, crossing into Russia with a load of Bibles, speaking in South Africa when her strength had given out. She taught about the ministry of angels and said, "What can we expect from angels? I don't know in detail, but this I do believe: when a Christian dies, an angel will lead him or her to heaven. Lazarus was carried to heaven by the angels; just think how wonderful that must have been. But already now we need their help, and you can safely count on their being here."

When she was a child, she used to say these verses before she went to bed:

> There are fourteen angels with me,
> Two on my right side, two on my left side,
> Two at my head, two at my feet,
> Two covering me, two to wake me up,
> Two to guide me to paradise.

The poem may not be very biblical, but the assurance of protection is comforting.

How many times it is a chore to visit those who are sick or old. But to walk into Shalom House was to experience a joy and beauty that encouraged the visitors. A neighbor, Maurine Parrott, said, "God's love and peace have continued to radiate through Corrie to us and to others, even since her illness, though she is paralyzed and cannot speak."

As the months stretched into years and the great communicator remained mute, her body gradually becoming weaker as age and successive strokes took their toll, the lessons to be learned from this last phase of her long life became clearer. Through her example and the loving care of those who surrounded her, we were able to see God's view of a human life. She was making an important statement in this humanistic world: that however limited physical circumstances may be, human life is made in the image of God, is precious and worth living.

One of the reasons Corrie remained as vibrant as she was, in spite of the final months when she was unable to move or speak, was because of her lifelong caring for others. Pam told of times when she would point toward the door, trying to make them understand her concern for someone. Lotte and Pam would attempt to discover the object of her thoughts by playing a form of Twenty Questions, until they would guess that she was thinking about someone who had written a troubled letter or a missionary she had in her mind. Then they would pray for that person and Corrie would visibly relax.

Pam said, "This kind of communication takes place often, and the Lord helps us constantly. Those of us who take care of Tante Corrie count it a great privilege."

The fear of growing old is combined in the human heart with the dread of becoming useless. A lifetime of service need not end when one is physically incapacitated. The visitors who left Corrie's bedside saw a peace that "passes all understanding." Many said that if she could be joyful in the Lord in her circumstances, then they surely could be in theirs.

On several occasions, Pam and Lotte would hear Corrie laughing with pure joy.

Why does God allow suffering? Those closest to Corrie said, "In His love, God has allowed this present suffering, and although suffering in itself is not a good thing, through it He is being glorified. We believe, although she cannot tell us, that she is seeing something of His glory while she awaits the very best that is yet to be."

Glory is as mystical as it is tangible. To describe it, man is inadequate; to experience it, lives can be changed. God's glory is one of life's great mysteries that will be completely understood in eternity. It was present in the bedroom where an old woman, her once-robust body just a frail shell, her face pale and fragile like a lovely piece of porcelain, lay quietly. One visitor said, "The room was inundated with a beauty that I cannot express. Tante Corrie is abiding in the foyer of heaven. Any day now she will be entering in. But as with Paul, who was caught up into the third heaven, I am sure that she has been there in her spirit for some time."

In the last active years of her life, Corrie's messages contained a strong prophetic nature. Against the gathering storm of worldwide unrest, crashing morality, and secular humanism, she believed the time was short before the Second Coming.

Her name may never be remembered in secular history, but God's history book is somewhat different. One Dutch friend wrote, "The real history of our time will be written by the Holy Spirit. Some names in that new history will ring out, and I can imagine that in that book there will be a whole chapter saying: 'In that time in the lowlands there stood up a prophetess in the name of the Lord, called Fruitful Tree [*ten Boom* means "tree" in Dutch], who spoke to the people, saying, "Return to the Lord, you backsliding people, for His day is near." '

" 'But the people did not listen to her, for the Lord had hardened their hearts, and the Lord sent her overseas to a people who received her message with gladness of heart. For a prophet is seldom honored in his own land.' "

God spoke to Corrie through His Book, the Bible, just as He has spoken to generations of believers and is still speaking today. He also spoke to her through her family, through dreams and visions, and through her constant prayer communication.

The last vision she had of God's speaking to her was one that electrifies those who have heard the story. We can either shrug away her words as those of a fantasying old woman or consider them as a prophetic sign from a person who, for almost a century, lived in close communication with the Lord.

About six months before she became ill, Corrie hurried down the hall to Pam's room late one evening.

She had been reading a book about the glory of God and longed for more of that quality to be revealed to her. On the night the Lord spoke to her, she told Pam, "I asked the Lord to see more of His glory, and He assured me that I would. Then I asked the Lord what we are longing to know. I said, 'Lord, are you coming soon?' "

As she sat on Pam's bed that night, she told of the answer the Lord gave her. "The Lord told me that first I would go to heaven, and then very shortly after He would come again."

What is God saying through His servant? Perhaps the strongest message Corrie would give to us in this latter part of the twentieth century would be, "If He is coming soon, we should be ready. The best is yet to be."

And the Bible says, "Remember those who led you, who spoke the word of God to you; and considering the outcome of their way of life, imitate their faith" (Hebrews 13:7).

Someday we will see the whole of the world's history. In Corrie's life we have seen God's plan.

Epilogue

Corrie ten Boom

April 15, 1892, Amsterdam, Holland–
April 15, 1983, Placentia, California

Corrie celebrated her ninety-first birthday in heaven. After almost five years of physical inactivity, she quietly left her earthly body to join the Lord she served and the people she loved.

She had wasted to a frail shell of her once-robust self, but in spite of pain in her last days, Corrie was a constant reminder of the sanctity of life and God's sovereign plan for His children.

If she could have spoken, she would have reminded us that, "Now we know that if the earthly tent we live in is destroyed, we have a building from God, an eternal house in heaven. . . . Meanwhile we groan, longing to be clothed with our heavenly dwelling . . . (2 Corinthians 5:1, 2 NIV).

At her memorial services her favorite Bach chorales sounded through the small, fragrant chapel. A few friends, representing the millions of lives she had touched, listened to tributes from Chuck Smith, her pastor; William Barbour, her publisher; and Cliff Barrows, her dear friend.

As the congregation sang the last stanza of that familiar old hymn, it was an appropriate finis to the earthly life of Corrie ten Boom:

> Stand up, stand up for Jesus, the strife will not be long
> This day the noise of battle—the next the victor's song;
> To him that overcometh A crown of life shall be:
> He with the King of glory Shall reign eternally.

What did Corrie leave? Very few possessions of monetary value could be included in her estate. Book and film royalties are being used for her worldwide ministries, which will continue long after her passing. However, the inheritance she bequeathed is rich in the messages of forgiveness, love, and warning.

She has told us that Jesus is coming soon. Will that make a difference in the way we live?

Source Notes

1. Helen Colijn, *Of Dutch Ways* (Minneapolis: Dillon, 1980), p. 211.
2. Kenneth La Tourette, *Christianity in a Revolutionary Age: A History of Christianity in the Nineteenth and Twentieth Centuries* (Grand Rapids: Zondervan, 1959), vol. 1, *The Nineteenth Century in Europe.*
3. Corrie ten Boom, *Father ten Boom: God's Man* (Old Tappan, N.J.: Fleming H. Revell, 1978), p. 29.
4. *Ibid.,* p. 32.
5. *Ibid.,* p. 33.
6. *Ibid.,* p. 43.
7. H. R. H. Wilhelmina, *Lonely But Not Alone* (New York: McGraw-Hill, 1959), p. 58.
8. ten Boom, *Father ten Boom,* p. 51.
9. *Ibid.,* pp. 64, 65.
10. *Ibid.,* pp. 98, 99.
11. H. R. H. Wilhelmina, *Lonely But Not Alone,* pp. 80, 81.
12. *Ibid.,* p. 90
13. Max Schuchart, *The Netherlands* (New York: Walker and Co., 1972).
14. H. R. H. Wilhelmina, *Lonely But Not Alone,* p. 147.
15. *Ibid.,* p. 151.
16. Colijn, *Of Dutch Ways,* p. 51.
17. Werner Warmbrunn, *The Dutch Under German Occupation* (Stanford, Calif: Stanford University Press, 1963), p. 44, 52.
18. Colijn, *Of Dutch Ways,* p. 50.
19. *Ibid.,* p. 52.
20. H. R. H. Wilhelmina, *Lonely But Not Alone,* p. 19.
21. Warmbrunn, *The Dutch Under German Occupation.*
22. Viktor Frankl, *Man's Search for Meaning* (Boston: Beacon Press, 1959), p. 11.
23. H. R. H. Wilhemina, *Lonely But Not Alone,* p. 161.
24. Colijn, *Of Dutch Ways,* p. 59.
25. Ellen de Kroon Stamps, *My Years With Corrie* (Old Tappan, N.J.: Fleming H. Revell, 1978), p. 47.
26. *Ibid.*
27. Corrie ten Boom, *Marching Orders for the End Battle* (Fort Washington, Penn.: Christian Literature Crusade, 1970).
28. Corrie ten Boom, *A Tramp Finds a Home* (Old Tappan, N.J.: Fleming H. Revell, 1978), p. 51.
29. Herbert Lockyer, *All the Women of the Bible* (Grand Rapids: Zondervan, 1977) p. 30.